Way of the Star

A Guided Advent Journal for Prayer and Meditation

Andrea Thomas and Greg Boudreaux

Nihil Obstat: Reverend Monsignor Michael Heintz, PhD
Censor Librorum
Imprimatur: Most Reverend Kevin C. Rhoades
Bishop of Fort Wayne–South Bend
Given at Fort Wayne, Indiana, on April 29, 2026

Cover and interior art created by Natalie Haydel Barker (colorsbynatalie.art) for the album *Way of the Star*.

Founded in 1865, Ave Maria Press is a ministry of the United States Province of Holy Cross.

www.avemariapress.com

Paperback: ISBN-13 978-1-64680-500-6

E-book: ISBN-13 978-1-64680-501-3

Cover and text design by Brianna Dombo Nicholson.

Printed and bound in the United States of America.

GET THE FULL EXPERIENCE WITH **FREE** COMPANION RESOURCES AND VIDEOS

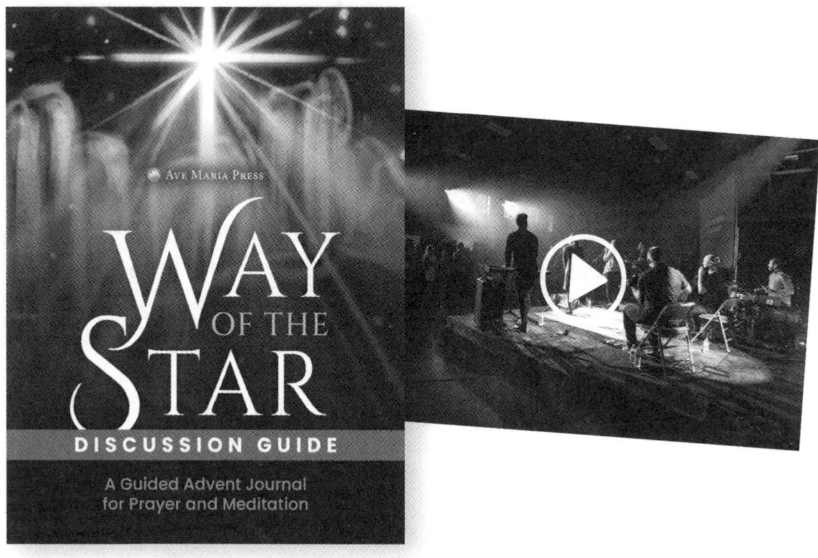

As you begin your Advent journey, don't forget to access these **FREE** resources for a truly immersive experience.

- Inspiring companion videos
- *The Way of the Star Discussion Guide*
- Beautiful art and music from The Vigil Project
- and more!

Scan here to access the free resources and videos, or visit **avemariapress.com/pages/way-of-the-star-resources**.

Dedicated to the community in Modena, Italy, with gratitude for sparking in us the original inspiration for *Way of the Star*.

CONTENTS

OCTAVE OF CHRISTMAS: EMMANUEL, GOD WITH US

INTRODUCTION

The Vigil Project

Ten years ago, a group of friends with musical talent and a common call to serve the Church gathered to record an album for Lent and Easter. We never would have guessed that the simple beginning to our story as a Catholic music apostolate would lead us down a path that would include the writing of this book as well as the many other projects and events we have been part of. When we allow God to write the story, he authors what no one else could ever think of.

Far from simply being a touring band, the Vigil Project is a small team of dedicated Catholics on a mission—each member deeply talented in his or her own right—to make music for the Catholic journey of faith. We write and play music with a true Catholic ethos so that Jesus is the name that is lifted higher. You will experience some of that music as a key part of our journey together this Advent. We also work tirelessly to assist Catholic musicians who serve at the parish and diocesan levels, with the

The Vigil Project team from left to right: Tyler Neil, Cortney Eusea, Greg Boudreaux, Lizzy Boudreaux, Sophie Salopek, Andrea Thomas, Andrew Ferguson, and Andrew Goldstein

goal of reviving excellence in the sung prayer of the Church. Though most of the music we create is intended for devotional prayer, we desire to help the Church fully receive the big, beautiful, complex gift of music that God has given us for the purpose of growing in communion with him and with one another.

The words in this book were indeed written by specific people, but the fact that it was able to be written at all is the direct result of a team that works together in true friendship and self-sacrificing creative collaboration. All of the insights and ideas you will encounter have been drawn from the shared heart of a community that strives to move as one body, putting aside ego and competition to make something greater than the sum of its parts. When you read it, you will hear from all of us in some way. Our aim with this book is the same as that of all our projects: to facilitate authentic encounter with Jesus through the beauty of the arts.

Way of the Star

Before it was the title of this book, *Way of the Star* was a music album we wrote for Advent and Christmas. It is a unique album, both in its origin and its form—it actually first took shape as a project for a live event in Modena, Italy. After years of receiving the most generous outpourings of hospitality from a small community of friends there who love our music, we wanted to write something as a gift to them that would remove the language barrier present in the English lyrics of our songs. We created something that unfolds similarly to the timeless devotion of the Stations of the Cross, only instead of telling the story of Christ's passion, *Way of the Star* tells the story of his infancy narrative in five scripturally based "stations." We used music to meditate on this story and combined it with dynamic visual art to facilitate a deep experience of imaginative prayer. We consider this book as not an afterthought to the project but rather a necessary completion of it.

A Journey of Listening

> To listen is to welcome
> the other into one's heart.
> —Cardinal Robert Sarah, *The Power of Silence*

The aim of our journey together through this Advent season is to grow in our capacity to listen to and hear the voice of God. Becoming better listeners will help us pray more deeply and recognize that we do not pray in a vacuum—we pray in a relationship. There is indeed an *other*—God—listening on the other side of our prayer. Learning to listen makes authentic relationships possible, whether that's with someone we are meeting for the first time or someone we already know really well. How else are we to truly encounter someone if we are not willing to receive them with an intentional decision to listen to them? How else are we to grow in deeper intimacy with someone except by our sustained, decisive listening?

In fact, one of the clearest ways to define a practice of prayer is simply to name it as our life of relationship with the Father, Son, and Holy Spirit. Sometimes we approach prayer as something other than that:

The community in Vignola, Italy, gathers in the parish church to pray and experience the music and artwork of *Way of the Star*.

- Maybe we think of it as a sort of therapeutic practice to ease our stress.
- Maybe we think of it as a last resort in the face of our immediate problems.
- Maybe we think of it as a magic formula to ask for what we want.
- Maybe we think of it as a transactional exchange in which if I do "this," God will do "that."
- Maybe we think of it as a purely duty-driven ritual.

Indeed, some of the things on this list are part of prayer or a result of it, but none of them even come close to encompassing the heart of our relationship with God. Whatever we have made of prayer, the reality of what it is remains always the same: "Prayer is the living relationship of the children of God with their Father who is good beyond measure, with his Son Jesus Christ and with the Holy Spirit" (*CCC*, 2565). Maybe this is the first time you have ever heard this definition; maybe you have heard it many times before. In either case, the reality of what God has invited us into in the relationship of prayer should reach our ears like a great song that is always worth hearing again.

If we are ever tempted to think ourselves so familiar with the heart of prayer, and thus the heart of God, that we pass quickly over this fundamental truth, perhaps we will find a special invitation in this blessed Advent season with all of its familiar traditions and stories. We are not merely entering into this

> It is our perennial spiritual and psychological task to look at things that are familiar until they become unfamiliar again.
> —G. K. Chesterton

> When man comes into contact with God, mere speech is not enough. Areas of his existence are awakened that spontaneously turn into song.
> —Cardinal Joseph Ratzinger, ***The Spirit of the Liturgy***

season because the calendar says it is time to do so. If this is our disposition, we risk letting Advent itself go in one ear and out the other. We enter this season with the faith that the heart of God given—spoken—to us in the Word Made Flesh is entirely inexhaustible for us. We enter this season with the humility to listen again, knowing that there remain heights and depths we have yet to see in the perfect love of our God who makes all things—even familiar things—new.

This Advent provides us with an opportunity to attune our listening to authentic prayer. As we journey together through these weeks, we will hear a story that hinges on how real people listened to the voice of God. Mary, Joseph, the shepherds, the Magi, and even Herod all teach us something about how God speaks and how he calls us to listen. Whether we have heard it a thousand times before or never before, when we listen deeply for the voice of the Lord speaking to us through the scriptural story of his infancy, we will be transformed, for he promises to meet us here. Because he is God's Word, we encounter Christ in these words that have been handed down to us in sacred scripture.

The way we will listen in prayer together in this Advent journey will likely be both familiar and unlike any way you have prayed before. We will read the words of scripture on the page, but we will also listen to them expressed in music and see them portrayed in art. In all of these movements, we will remain in the posture of *listening*—a posture of receptivity, a posture of wonder. As we follow the way of the star this Advent, perhaps we will discover an untapped capacity to hear God and thus encounter our Savior Jesus, again or for the first time, as never before.

HOW TO USE THIS JOURNAL

This book functions as the centerpiece of a multimedia experience of imaginative prayer and meditation. While the text of this book stands on its own as a valuable resource for prayer without its parallel elements, we intend for it to be experienced together with the music and artwork provided as different ways to be drawn into deeper listening. For example, instead of simply reading the scriptures, we invite you to listen to them by seeing the words on the page, listening to the expression of them in music, and gazing on the depiction of them in art. All of these encounters become opportunities for us to listen in gradually increasing depth.

Each week of this journey will focus on one of five key passages in Jesus's infancy narrative, the story of how Christ's birth came about. We will begin each week on Sunday with a full passage from scripture, experiencing this part of the story in a variety of media (reading, music, and art). Gradually over the course of the week, Monday through Friday, we will listen more closely to each line of this scripture passage, one or two verses per day, to mine the depths of what God is speaking to us. Each day's prayer will unfold with repeating cues in this book:

- **Listen**: This section presents the words of scripture for you to read.
- **Listen Again**: These prompts invite you to engage your imagination in prayer—to "listen" to the words of scripture and meditate on some key questions about the scene.
- **Ponder**: This brief reflection offers some insights in response to the text we have taken in that day. This section was written by Andrea Thomas and is drawn from the fruit of her own listening to these passages.

- **Reflect and Pray**: These questions serve as a launching point for your personal response of prayer to what you have heard and experienced in the scripture passages. You are invited to write your own words of prayer in a time of journaling.

Each *week* will also unfold with its own rhythm:

- **Sundays** include all of the elements above, in addition to artwork depicting the scene from scripture for the week. You will also see a QR code and website link in Sunday posts that invite you to watch a video with Andrea and me (Greg) speaking about the themes for the week and the ways they are represented in an original musical composition from the Vigil Project. After our introduction, the video will continue with the music.

- **Weekdays** are a time to journey through the scripture passage verse by verse in the "listen" and "listen again" process, which will help you use your imagination to engage with these scenes from the birth of Christ. We encourage you to return to the musical composition throughout the week.

- **Saturdays** will conclude each week by presenting the scripture passage again in its entirety—as it appears in text, music, and artwork—and inviting you to "mine the gems" of your prayer as you reflect on the insights and conclusions you have reached in the past six days. In this way, we will experience and gather up the ways our listening has deepened our understanding and our relationship with God. You'll also have the opportunity each week to view a video that puts the week's music and art together in a reflective animation. Our hope is that the music and images give you

Don't miss the QR code on Saturdays to view the weekly reflective video. You can also find them at www.avemariapress.com/pages/way-of-the-star-resources.

room to experience the fullness of each passage from scripture as an encounter with the living God.

This book provides ample space each day for journaling, so use the space to write down your thoughts and feelings or to record your prayer encounters with God. If journaling feels too open-ended for you, use the following template (which is pulled from the *Catechism of the Catholic Church*, 2708), and simply jot down notes as you bring each of these elements of yourself to the scriptural passage, reflection, and prayer:

- What do I **think**?
- What do I **imagine**?
- What do I **feel**?
- What do I **desire**?

Over time, it may be fruitful to review the progress of your Advent journey to see how God is meeting you in this experience.

No firm time limits apply to how you journey through this content each day, but be sure to give this prayer experience the space you need to step away from the world and into a posture of listening. Some days you may have less time to offer; other days you may feel like lingering—listening to those cues is a way to grow more attuned to how God is speaking with you through this experience.

You can work through this prayer experience on your own, with a friend or family member, with your whole family, or with a group at your parish. If making the journey with a prayer group that meets regularly, we recommend that the group pick a day

If you would like more structure to assist with a small group, you can find a free, downloadable guide in PDF form at www.avemariapress.com/pages/way-of-the-star-resources.

to meet weekly to pray together through the content and share aloud the insights you have captured in your journaling and prayer.

If you miss a day, be encouraged to stay the course and continue to move at your own pace through the meditations. If the Holy Spirit invites you to move ahead or stay still in a specific meditation for longer, follow those promptings. Our prayer is not a race to a prize—it is a relationship, which is itself the reward. The Holy Spirit teaches us to pray as we ought (see Romans 8:26–27). Let us fully open our hearts to God's promptings along the way—he is the one we are learning to listen and respond to. We can have every confidence that he is leading us, for this is the very reason he sent his Son to us.

> Meditation engages thought, imagination, emotion, and desire. This mobilization of faculties is necessary in order to deepen our convictions of faith, prompt the conversion of our heart, and strengthen our will to follow Christ.
>
> —***Catechism of the Catholic Church***, 2708

FIRST WEEK OF ADVENT

MARY, HANDMAID OF THE LORD

FIRST WEEK OF ADVENT

SUNDAY

Listen: Luke 1:26–38

The angel Gabriel was sent from God to a town of Galilee called Nazareth, to a virgin betrothed to a man named Joseph, of the house of David, and the virgin's name was Mary. And coming to her, he said, "Hail, favored one! The Lord is with you." But she was greatly troubled at what was said and pondered what sort of greeting this might be. Then the angel said to her, "Do not be afraid, Mary, for you have found favor with God. Behold, you will conceive in your womb and bear a son, and you shall name him Jesus. He will be great and will be called Son of the Most High, and the Lord God will give him the throne of David his father, and he will rule over the house of Jacob forever, and of his kingdom there will be no end." But Mary said to the angel, "How can this be, since I have no relations with a man?" And the angel said to her in reply, "The holy Spirit will come upon you, and the power of the Most High will overshadow you. Therefore the child to be born will be called holy, the Son of God. . . . For nothing will be impossible for God." Mary said, "Behold, I am the handmaid of the Lord. May it be done to me according to your word." Then the angel departed from her.

Listen Again

Listen to "Mary, Handmaid of the Lord," which can be found at the link below.

In the absence of words to listen to in the music, pay attention to what the instruments are "speaking." Listen for the way the violin expresses the interior thoughts and feelings of Mary as she dialogues with the angel. Listen to how the cello dances melodically with the violin, imagining the movement of the Holy Spirit as Mary's spouse. Listen to how the human voices express outwardly the interior things that the strings emote as the moment of the annunciation arrives and the message is declared to Mary.

While you listen, look at the artwork for this week and allow your imagination to draw you into the scene. What is Mary doing just before the angel comes to her? Is she at prayer? What does the voice of the angel sound like? Why is Mary troubled by his greeting? As the angel departs and Mary again finds herself alone, what is she thinking? What is she feeling? What does she do?

Scan this code with your phone or visit www.avemariapress.com/pages/way-of-the-star-resources **to find a video introduction to this week's prayer themes and a recording of "Mary, Handmaid of the Lord."**

Ponder: O Night Divine

At one time or another, we've all heard that God's timing is perfect. I must admit that when this reminder is presented to me, I have one of two reactions: I am either grateful, and a slight smile comes to my face, or I am viscerally irritated. To us, sometimes God's timing feels right, and sometimes—in the shattered valley of tears we call our earthly home—God's timing feels very, very wrong.

Long lay the world in sin
and error pining . . .

As we begin this Advent journey and open our hearts to the story of Jesus's birth, we find ourselves sitting with Our Lady at the epicenter of God's appointed time to send a Savior to rescue a broken world. For many generations, the Chosen People had been waiting with aching hearts, pining for a savior, desperate for things to be different. Even Mary herself, knowing that the Messiah was foretold, knew not the day nor the hour of his arrival. Gabriel could have been sent by God at any moment in history, but his arrival to her is the time that God had deemed perfect. And Mary discovered that when God breaks through our circumstances, everything changes in an instant.

Hebrews 4:12 tells us that "the word of God is living and effective, sharper than any two-edged sword, penetrating even between soul and spirit, joints and marrow, and able to discern reflections and thoughts of the heart." Have you ever gone to Mass and discovered the readings presenting the perfect message for where you found yourself that day? Or opened your Bible and turned to the perfect scripture passage for the scenario you were living through? I am not advocating for discernment to be reduced to a game of spiritual roulette, but I am saying that God's Word very much still speaks to us. The Word was made flesh and made his dwelling among us. When we encounter the words of scripture, we are encountering Jesus himself, the Word of God.

So, on this first Sunday of the first week of Advent, perhaps we can open our hearts to the possibility that God will pierce through our circumstances in the way that he deems best over the next several weeks and into the Christmas octave. Perhaps we can ask the Blessed Mother to help us yield completely to the Holy Spirit, just as she did, and let it be done to us according to God's will.

Respond

1. When you ponder the fact that God has perfect timing, what reaction arises in you? What moments from your life come to mind that support or reject this notion of God's perfect timing? What do you want to ask God about his timing?
2. What are your hopes for this Advent? What kind of growth are you being called to in this season?
3. Ask God what he wants you to know and watch for as you begin this Advent season.

FIRST WEEK OF ADVENT

MONDAY

Listen: Luke 1:26–28

In the sixth month, the angel Gabriel was sent from God to a town of Galilee called Nazareth, to a virgin betrothed to a man named Joseph, of the house of David, and the virgin's name was Mary. And coming to her, he said, "Hail, favored one! The Lord is with you." But she was greatly troubled at what was said and pondered what sort of greeting this might be. Then the angel said to her, "Do not be afraid, Mary, for you have found favor with God. Behold, you will conceive in your womb and bear a son, and you shall name him Jesus. He will be great and will be called Son of the Most High, and the Lord God will give him the throne of David his father, and he will rule over the house of Jacob forever, and of his kingdom there will be no end." But Mary said to the angel, "How can this be, since I have no relations with a man?" And the angel said to her in reply, "The holy Spirit will come upon you, and the power of the Most High will overshadow you. Therefore the child to be born will be called holy, the Son of God. . . . For nothing will be impossible for God." Mary said, "Behold, I am the handmaid of the Lord. May it be done to me according to your word." Then the angel departed from her. (Lk 1:26–38)

Listen Again

As you begin to meditate on the bolded verses above, engage your imagination and use the following questions to enter deeply into the scene. From where was the angel Gabriel sent? To where was he sent? What time of day does this encounter take place? What does the room look like? What happens at the moment of Gabriel's appearance as he comes to Mary?

Ponder: St. Augustine and *How the Grinch Stole Christmas*

The amount of time that the Chosen People had to wait for the foretold Savior really depends on when you start counting. Whether you begin counting from the first announcement of the Good News in the Garden of Eden or from the promise to Abraham that marked the beginning of the Chosen People, we're talking thousands of years. And then in an instant, Jesus comes to us through the announcement of the angel Gabriel and our Blessed Mother's yes to God's invitation.

St. Augustine believed that periods of waiting—especially *long* periods of waiting—expand our hearts. As our desire grows, the capacity of our hearts is increased to receive more of what God wants to give us. And while in the long run this stretching is a great gift, it can be excruciatingly painful.

The growth God invites us to often makes me think of Jim Carrey's depiction of the Grinch in *How the Grinch Stole Christmas*. Toward the end of the movie, we listen as the narrator says, "Then the Grinch thought of something he hadn't before: 'Maybe Christmas,' he thought, 'doesn't come from a store. Maybe Christmas perhaps means a little bit more.' And what happened then, well, in Whoville they say that the Grinch's small heart grew three sizes that day." The Grinch then dramatically grips his heart and falls to the ground, wailing in pain. Carrey's performance is actually profoundly accurate to the human experience. He goes from hardened, angry, and closed off to softened, joyful, and sobbing. The reason for this? His heart expanded when he opened himself to the gift of love, and he was then able to receive *more* of the gift. He experienced beauty and pain all at the same time.

Advent is a word that means "waiting," but this is not just a passive waiting. This season carries with it an expectant waiting, a hopefulness, an anticipation of someone who is coming—almost as if you're at the front door on the lookout for someone to pull into your driveway whom you know is just around the corner. Our lives are full of advents, but God does not allow us to wait in vain. The waiting he invites us to do is always filled with great purpose and oriented to growing our desire for him.

Respond

1. What are you waiting on God for right now?
2. How can you entrust your waiting to God? How might he be at work in your life to expand your heart as he desires, even if it's uncomfortable or even painful?
3. Ask God to increase your patience and your desire for the gifts he wants to give.

FIRST WEEK OF ADVENT

TUESDAY

Listen: Luke 1:29–30

In the sixth month, the angel Gabriel was sent from God to a town of Galilee called Nazareth, to a virgin betrothed to a man named Joseph, of the house of David, and the virgin's name was Mary. And coming to her, he said, "Hail, favored one! The Lord is with you." **But she was greatly troubled at what was said and pondered what sort of greeting this might be. Then the angel said to her, "Do not be afraid, Mary, for you have found favor with God.** Behold, you will conceive in your womb and bear a son, and you shall name him Jesus. He will be great and will be called Son of the Most High, and the Lord God will give him the throne of David his father, and he will rule over the house of Jacob forever, and of his kingdom there will be no end." But Mary said to the angel, "How can this be, since I have no relations with a man?" And the angel said to her in reply, "The holy Spirit will come upon you, and the power of the Most High will overshadow you. Therefore the child to be born will be called holy, the Son of God. . . . For nothing will be impossible for God." Mary said, "Behold, I am the handmaid of the Lord. May it be done to me according to your word." Then the angel departed from her. (Lk 1:26–38)

Listen Again

As you begin to meditate on the bolded scripture above, engage your imagination and use the following questions to enter deeply into the scene. What is Mary feeling as the angel appears to her and begins to speak? What is the temperature of the room? Why is she troubled by his message that "the Lord is with you"? Is she afraid? How does it make her feel when he says, "You have found favor with God"?

Ponder: It Is the Whole Man Who Prays

St. Thomas Aquinas teaches us that grace builds on nature: Grace from God does not replace our humanity; rather, it *elevates* our humanity.

The Advent season invites us to reflect on the reality that God chose to become one of us in order to bring us into communion with him, even though he had an infinite number of other ways he could have chosen to save us. His very name—Emmanuel—means "God with us." He loves us so profoundly that he took onto himself every element of our humanity except sin—things like thought, imagination, emotion, and desire. These faculties we possess are great gifts, and the *Catechism* tells us that we are meant to engage with them, in both our everyday life in the world and our interior life.

> It is the whole man who prays.
> —***Catechism of the Catholic Church***, 2562

Mary was "greatly troubled" by Gabriel's message, but God did not dismiss her feelings. Rather, Gabriel assured her to "not be afraid." God does not ask us to set any part of ourselves aside as we approach him—he wants to meet us in the fullness of who we are.

Respond

Look at today's scripture passage and bring the whole of yourself—all of your faculties—to this time of prayer.

1. Thought: Think about what Mary might have been doing when the angel Gabriel arrived. What activity was she coming from or going to?
2. Imagination: Imagine yourself in the room where Mary is. Where is she? What is her posture? Where are you?
3. Emotion: How is Mary feeling? Really try to study her in the scene. What is the expression on her face? How are you feeling? Can you identify why?
4. Desire: What would you like to ask Mary? Is there anything you'd like to share with her? Take a moment to approach her in prayer and ask for her help this Advent.

FIRST WEEK OF ADVENT

WEDNESDAY

Listen: Luke 1:31–33

In the sixth month, the angel Gabriel was sent from God to a town of Galilee called Nazareth, to a virgin betrothed to a man named Joseph, of the house of David, and the virgin's name was Mary. And coming to her, he said, "Hail, favored one! The Lord is with you." But she was greatly troubled at what was said and pondered what sort of greeting this might be. Then the angel said to her, "Do not be afraid, Mary, for you have found favor with God. **Behold, you will conceive in your womb and bear a son, and you shall name him Jesus. He will be great and will be called Son of the Most High, and the Lord God will give him the throne of David his father, and he will rule over the house of Jacob forever, and of his kingdom there will be no end."** But Mary said to the angel, "How can this be, since I have no relations with a man?" And the angel said to her in reply, "The holy Spirit will come upon you, and the power of the Most High will overshadow you. Therefore the child to be born will be called holy, the Son of God. . . . For nothing will be impossible for God." Mary said, "Behold, I am the handmaid of the Lord. May it be done to me according to your word." Then the angel departed from her. (Lk 1:26–38)

Listen Again

As you begin to meditate on the bolded scripture above, engage your imagination and use the following questions to enter deeply into the scene. Imagine you have never heard these words before and encounter Gabriel's message to Mary as if for the first time. How do they strike you? What do they mean to you? Do you believe them?

Ponder: Expectations

Many couples have told me over the years that their spouse was not someone they expected they would marry. I recently had a friend tell me the story of his brother deciding one night he would surrender "his type" to God and come to him with open hands and an open heart. The very next day he woke up seeing a friend of his with new eyes, a friend who—you guessed it—became his wife. The conclusion from these couples seems to be the same: If I didn't allow for my expectations to be shattered or shifted, I could have missed the greatest blessing of my life.

We have established that the Jewish people were long awaiting their Savior. The general expectation was that he would be a powerful military leader who would lead them out from under Roman occupation and establish a powerful, dominant, earthly kingdom. But instead of a royal palace, Jesus came in a humble stable. Instead of an earthly kingdom, Jesus tells us that his kingdom is not of this world (see John 18:36). He came to save us not by government military dominion but by waging spiritual battle.

There were many who simply could not accept that the Savior would come in a way different from their expectations. And they rejected him. How hard it can be to let go of our expectations. How difficult it can be to allow God to shatter or shift them and accept what he offers us—what he knows is best.

Respond

1. What expectations do you carry about how you look for God to show up in your life? Where do those expectations come from? God is much bigger than the categories we have for him, so how might he be reaching for you in unexpected ways?
2. How can you grow in your willingness to lay down your expectations and simply offer God open hands and an open heart?
3. Ask God to help you trust him enough to believe that wherever he leads you is going to be toward a fuller, richer, more abundant life.

FIRST WEEK OF ADVENT

THURSDAY

Listen: Luke 1:34–37

In the sixth month, the angel Gabriel was sent from God to a town of Galilee called Nazareth, to a virgin betrothed to a man named Joseph, of the house of David, and the virgin's name was Mary. And coming to her, he said, "Hail, favored one! The Lord is with you." But she was greatly troubled at what was said and pondered what sort of greeting this might be. Then the angel said to her, "Do not be afraid, Mary, for you have found favor with God. Behold, you will conceive in your womb and bear a son, and you shall name him Jesus. He will be great and will be called Son of the Most High, and the Lord God will give him the throne of David his father, and he will rule over the house of Jacob forever, and of his kingdom there will be no end." **But Mary said to the angel, "How can this be, since I have no relations with a man?" And the angel said to her in reply, "The holy Spirit will come upon you, and the power of the Most High will overshadow you. Therefore the child to be born will be called holy, the Son of God. . . . For nothing will be impossible for God."** Mary said, "Behold, I am the handmaid of the Lord. May it be done to me according to your word." Then the angel departed from her. (Lk 1:26–38)

Listen Again

As you begin to meditate on the bolded scripture above, engage your imagination and use the following questions to enter deeply into the scene. Imagine that you are in the room near Mary as she begins to converse with the angel. What expression is on her face? What disposition is Mary's question coming from when she asks, "How can this be?" Doubt? Trust? Fear? Faith? Something else? How do you see her disposition affected when the angel answers her question?

Ponder: Asking Great Things

The vast majority of Jesus's recorded miracles concluded with him saying something along the lines of "Your faith has saved you." The miracles he performed were truly impossible feats—but nothing is impossible for God. The blind could then see, the deaf could hear, the leper was made clean, the dead were raised back to life, many hearts were converted, those bound by demons were healed, and other people of his time witnessed many more signs and wonders. In many cases, Jesus emphasized that their trust in him was actually the catalyst for their healing. The disposition of the heart of the one experiencing the miracle really mattered. They believed he could change their lives, and further, they believed he *would*. Do we carry the same willingness to believe?

Do we get every miracle that we pray for? No, we don't—and there's a challenging mystery in that reality. But to quote St. Teresa of Avila, "You pay God a compliment by asking great things of him." We know that even if he doesn't answer us in the way we expect, or respond in the timing we desire, he is still good and working for our highest good. Miracle or not, the disposition of our hearts toward him matters.

Respond

1. We have all heard that nothing is impossible for God, but what gets in the way of my belief that this is true for me in my own life? What parts of my life feel impossible right now?
2. Now that we have cultivated nearly a week of prayer, what do you notice about the disposition of your heart in these encounters?
3. Ask God to help you grow in confidence in his love for you and his great care for the circumstances in your life.

FIRST WEEK OF ADVENT

FRIDAY

Listen: Luke 1:38

In the sixth month, the angel Gabriel was sent from God to a town of Galilee called Nazareth, to a virgin betrothed to a man named Joseph, of the house of David, and the virgin's name was Mary. And coming to her, he said, "Hail, favored one! The Lord is with you." But she was greatly troubled at what was said and pondered what sort of greeting this might be. Then the angel said to her, "Do not be afraid, Mary, for you have found favor with God. Behold, you will conceive in your womb and bear a son, and you shall name him Jesus. He will be great and will be called Son of the Most High, and the Lord God will give him the throne of David his father, and he will rule over the house of Jacob forever, and of his kingdom there will be no end." But Mary said to the angel, "How can this be, since I have no relations with a man?" And the angel said to her in reply, "The holy Spirit will come upon you, and the power of the Most High will overshadow you. Therefore the child to be born will be called holy, the Son of God. . . . For nothing will be impossible for God." **Mary said, "Behold, I am the handmaid of the Lord. May it be done to me according to your word." Then the angel departed from her.** (Lk 1:26–38)

Listen Again

As you begin to meditate on the bolded scripture above, engage your imagination and use the following questions to enter deeply into the scene. What allows Mary to respond with such a radical yes in this moment? In what other moments of her life might she have offered a yes such as this one? As the angel stands before her, do you think she feels any temptation to respond in a way other than this? What is she thinking and feeling as the angel departs from her and Jesus is conceived in her womb?

Ponder: Trusting God with Open Hands

Think of what it is like to hold sand. In order to actually hold a quantity of sand, your hand must be fully open so that it can rest in a pile on your palm. If you try to clench the sand and grab onto it, it will fall right through your fingers back down to the earth. Someone once shared this image with me as a way to depict what it looks like when openness to God's will meets our free will.

God is never outdone in his generosity to us. We also can't pretend for a moment that we understand his ways, which are much higher than ours. We must choose whether we will trust him, especially in moments when we don't understand.

Mary's yes was total. There were no strings attached whatsoever. In her yes, she trusted God with her entire being, and she submitted all of herself to him. Her hands were perfectly open to whatever God desired to place in them.

Respond

1. What are the situations in your life where you try to grasp control? How might you also approach God with open hands to receive what he has to offer you in this experience?
2. In what specific part of your life or place in your heart is God asking you for a total surrender, a total yes this Advent?

3. Bring Mary's words to God in prayer as your own: "May it be done to me according to your word."

FIRST WEEK OF ADVENT

SATURDAY

Return and Recollect

Today, let us pause from our daily rhythm to reflect on what the Lord has done in and for us this week. Think of this as the moment of collecting the gems you have mined in prayer and meditation. Instead of laboring ahead, let us return to where we started to fully receive the gift of where we find ourselves today. While this might seem like an unnecessary repetition, be assured that pausing to look back is often when we discover the specific places and patterns in which God has been moving throughout our prayer.

Return and Listen: Luke 1:26–38

In the sixth month, the angel Gabriel was sent from God to a town of Galilee called Nazareth, to a virgin betrothed to a man named Joseph, of the house of David, and the virgin's name was Mary. And coming to her, he said, "Hail, favored one! The Lord is with you." But she was greatly troubled at what was said and pondered what sort of greeting this might be. Then the angel said to her, "Do not be afraid, Mary, for you have found favor with God. Behold, you will conceive in your womb and bear a son, and you shall name him Jesus. He will be great and will be called Son of the Most High, and the Lord God will give him the throne of David his father, and he will rule over the house of Jacob forever, and of his kingdom there will be no end." But Mary said to the angel, "How can this be, since I have no relations with a man?" And the angel said to her in reply, "The holy Spirit will come upon you, and the power of the Most High will overshadow you. Therefore the child to be born will be called holy, the Son of God. . . . For nothing will be impossible for God." Mary said, "Behold, I am the handmaid of the Lord. May it be done to me according to your word." Then the angel departed from her.

Return and Listen Again

Watch the animated video for "Mary, Handmaid of the Lord," which can be found at the link below.

As you encounter the music and artwork again in a more dynamic way, consider how your journey of imaginative prayer through this week has brought this part of the story more to life for you. What has God revealed to you that you had never considered before? What details of the scriptures have come to the surface? What images now exist in your mind's eye when you read these words?

Scan this code with your phone or visit www.avemariapress.com/pages/way-of-the-star-resources to view animated art and music for "Mary, Handmaid of the Lord."

Return and Respond

Collect your prayers from the week by reviewing your journaling notes and writing down anything that stands out to you. As you gather these "gems," pay attention to your own thoughts, feelings, and desires, and write down what you want to remember.

Also record here any new observations, continuing questions, or answered prayers that you notice. Take them to Mass with you this evening or tomorrow, and present them on the altar during your Sunday worship. Even as you respond in your journal to everything you have experienced this week, try to remain in a posture of listening for the promptings of the Holy Spirit as you go.

SECOND WEEK OF ADVENT

JOSEPH, RIGHTEOUS MAN

SECOND WEEK OF ADVENT

SUNDAY

Listen: Matthew 1:18–24

When his mother Mary was betrothed to Joseph, but before they lived together, she was found with child through the holy Spirit. Joseph her husband, since he was a righteous man, yet unwilling to expose her to shame, decided to divorce her quietly. Such was his intention when, behold, the angel of the Lord appeared to him in a dream and said, "Joseph, son of David, do not be afraid to take Mary your wife into your home. For it is through the holy Spirit that this child has been conceived in her. She will bear a son and you are to name him Jesus, because he will save his people from their sins." All this took place to fulfill what the Lord had said through the prophet:

"Behold, the virgin shall be with child and
bear a son,
and they shall name him Emmanuel,"

which means "God is with us." When Joseph awoke, he did as the angel of the Lord had commanded him and took his wife into his home.

Listen Again

Listen to "Joseph, Righteous Man," which can be found at the link below.

As you did last week, pay attention to the interaction of the voices, human and instrumental. See if you can imagine who and what they are expressing. In particular, notice how the "voices" of the violin and the cello now represent a conversation between Mary and Joseph. Also notice the dynamics and emotions of the music as they progress and shift from the beginning to the end: It starts off with a melody that feels heavy with grief. Then, this same melody is transformed into a decisive joy.

While you listen, look at the artwork at the beginning of this chapter and allow your imagination to draw you into the scene. How does Joseph find out that Mary is with child? How does this affect him? What thoughts about Mary fill his mind? What emotions is he wrestling with? Imagine where Joseph is sleeping when the angel comes to him in the dream. What does he see in the dream? What does he hear? When he wakes, how have his thoughts and emotions changed? Is he experiencing a new relief or peace? A deep joy? What does he do? What does he say to Mary when he sees her next?

Scan this code with your phone or visit www.avemariapress.com/pages/way-of-the-star-resources to find a video introduction to this week's prayer themes and a recording of "Joseph, Righteous Man."

Ponder: Loaves, Fishes, and Strep Throat

I remember well my first silent retreat. For a reason I cannot remotely recall, it seemed like a good idea to jump into a retreat that lasted eight days. I somehow chose not to ease in with something like a weekend retreat first—I went straight for the jugular with eight straight days. The priest preparing me shared some wise counsel prior to my departure: Silent retreats are as difficult to emerge from as they are to enter into. He also said I would likely be drawn to sleep a significant amount, especially the first few days.

He was right. The first few days I found myself sleeping upward of ten hours a day. I was tempted to think perhaps this was a sign of spiritual progression into the week and a green light that I was doing this right. Spoiler: It wasn't. I found out later I had full-blown strep throat and mononucleosis at the same time. I was sick as a dog and didn't have anybody to tell except for my spiritual director that week, and, figuring lethargy was just part of the experience, I chose not to say anything.

I remember going on a run and feeling a lump under my left rib cage, which was uncomfortable and odd but not super painful. I discovered later that it was, in fact, an enlarged spleen, which can develop when your body is fighting mono. The good news is that God can use human stupidity for great good. In my exhaustion and fatigue, my otherwise fiery nature was tempered, and I found that I was less resistant in my prayer and much more willing to yield to whatever God wanted to do. A less-than-optimal scenario of me being sick gave way to an incredibly fruitful retreat.

As we grab the matches to light the second candle of the Advent wreath today, I want to offer you a bit of encouragement. Sometimes, in our desire to do things well, we can gravitate toward the spirit of perfectionism. And if things aren't perfect, there can be a temptation to throw in the towel before you even get started on the journey.

Here is the truth, though: God can reveal something to you in a single instant that can change your trajectory, as he did to Joseph when he was sleeping. We simply do not know what God wants to do or say, or where he wants to lead us, and therefore we must not put God on any timetable or assume he is unable to work with any imperfect fragments of prayer we have to offer him.

If you feel inadequacy in prayer, I assure you that you are not alone. Much like the loaves and fishes, the Lord is pleased when we give him what we have to offer, even if it seems meager. It is up to him to multiply. Paul reminds us that "the Spirit too comes to the aid of our weakness; for we do not know how to pray as we ought" (Rom 8:26). Ask the Holy Spirit to help you pray as you ought this week. Offer him whatever loaves and fishes you have, and see what he does with them this week.

Respond

1. What limitations do you encounter in prayer? How do you feel insufficient in approaching God?
2. What does "perfect" prayer mean to you? What gets in the way of that kind of experience? Remember that prayer is relationship—God wants to share life with us more than he wants us to adhere to a routine, discipline, or certain practice. How can you draw on an awareness of God's nearness to you today?
3. Ask the Holy Spirit to help you more freely receive the gift of prayer.

SECOND WEEK OF ADVENT

MONDAY

Listen: Matthew 1:18–19

When his mother Mary was betrothed to Joseph, but before they lived together, she was found with child through the holy Spirit. Joseph her husband, since he was a righteous man, yet unwilling to expose her to shame, decided to divorce her quietly. Such was his intention when, behold, the angel of the Lord appeared to him in a dream and said, "Joseph, son of David, do not be afraid to take Mary your wife into your home. For it is through the holy Spirit that this child has been conceived in her. She will bear a son and you are to name him Jesus, because he will save his people from their sins." All this took place to fulfill what the Lord had said through the prophet:

> "Behold, the virgin shall be with child and
>   bear a son,
> and they shall name him Emmanuel,"

which means "God is with us." When Joseph awoke, he did as the angel of the Lord had commanded him and took his wife into his home. (Mt 1:18–24)

Listen Again

As you begin to meditate on the bolded scripture above, engage your imagination and use the following questions to enter deeply into the scene. Where do you imagine Joseph and Mary are standing as Mary shares with Joseph the news of her pregnancy? What is the conversation that ensues? What competing thoughts and emotions are running through Joseph's heart and mind as he hears the news and decides how to proceed—to divorce Mary quietly?

Ponder: St. Joseph and the Narrow Way

I sometimes think about how heartbroken St. Joseph must have been when he discovered that Mary was pregnant. Our knowledge of Joseph and Mary's relationship is limited, and we don't know how long they had been betrothed. We do know that betrothal back then was much more than engagement. It was a formal, legally binding agreement. Because he did not yet know the truth of Our Lady's miraculous pregnancy, this must have initially felt like the ultimate betrayal.

And what does he do? Joseph, in this critical moment, shows incredible virtue and unwavering trust in God. He was prepared to let Mary go and move on to whatever God had next for him. He showed deep compassion and love during a moment that, I can only imagine, felt like a crucible to him.

Joseph gives us an example of how to walk the narrow way, the path of righteousness. He shows us how to keep our eyes ever fixed on God, trusting in his providence no matter what happens. Joseph shows us what it looks like to trust that God is nearer than we imagine and directs our paths toward our good, even in what looks like an impossible situation.

Respond

1. Think of a situation in your life in which God is calling you to walk the narrow way of virtue and righteousness instead of the way of the world. How can you follow the faithful example of Joseph?
2. What gets in the way of trusting God fully, as Joseph did? How can you approach God with those insecurities and fears?
3. Ask God for the wisdom to navigate life with Joseph's humility and faithfulness.

SECOND WEEK OF ADVENT

TUESDAY

Listen: Matthew 1:20

When his mother Mary was betrothed to Joseph, but before they lived together, she was found with child through the holy Spirit. Joseph her husband, since he was a righteous man, yet unwilling to expose her to shame, decided to divorce her quietly. **Such was his intention when, behold, the angel of the Lord appeared to him in a dream and said, "Joseph, son of David, do not be afraid to take Mary your wife into your home. For it is through the holy Spirit that this child has been conceived in her.** She will bear a son and you are to name him Jesus, because he will save his people from their sins." All this took place to fulfill what the Lord had said through the prophet:

"Behold, the virgin shall be with child and
bear a son,
and they shall name him Emmanuel,"

which means "God is with us." When Joseph awoke, he did as the angel of the Lord had commanded him and took his wife into his home. (Mt 1:18–24)

Listen Again

As you begin to meditate on the bolded scripture above, engage your imagination and use the following questions to enter deeply into the scene. Imagine where Joseph is sleeping when the angel comes to him in the dream. What does he see in the dream? What does he hear? Like Mary, does he have questions for the angel? Or does he simply hear the proclamation?

Ponder: The Sleeping St. Joseph

The image of St. Joseph sleeping has become one of my favorite artistic depictions. It is such a rich reminder of the posture God desires for each one of us—a posture of rest.

I'll be the first to admit that I have struggled with the concept of rest. I have been quick to defend poor Martha in the scripture story of Mary and Martha in the Gospel of Luke. *Somebody* had to make lunch that day. These things don't just take care of themselves, right? But Jesus tells us it is not that Martha (who, for the record, is a canonized saint) did anything wrong but rather that Mary *chose the better part* (see Luke 10:42).

God does incredible work in the mystery of human rest. It's remarkable to consider that he created us to spend roughly one-third of our lives sleeping (insert laughs and eye rolls from parents with littles).

> Come to me, all you who labor and are burdened, and I will give you rest. Take my yoke upon you and learn from me, for I am meek and humble of heart; and you will find rest for yourselves. For my yoke is easy, and my burden light.
>
> —Matthew 11:28–30

Psalm 127 has also garnered a special place in my heart these last couple of years:

> Unless the LORD build the house,
> they labor in vain who build.
> Unless the LORD guard the city,
> in vain does the guard keep watch.
> It is vain for you to rise early
> and put off your rest at night,
> to eat bread earned by hard toil—
> all this God gives to his beloved in sleep.
> (Ps 127:1–2)

We live in a culture that eats many loaves of "the bread of hard toil." This is the antithesis of Jesus beckoning us to him to find rest for our souls (see Matthew 11:28–30). God redirected the course of Joseph's life—and thus, Jesus's and Mary's lives, too—in a moment of human rest. If you, too, struggle with rest, pray for the grace to trust that God is always at work, even (or perhaps especially) when we are not.

Respond

1. What do you most want the Lord to do for you? How do you want God to be present to you this Advent? Do you believe that he is *already* at work in your life and in your heart and that this work does not depend on your effort?
2. What makes you restless? What would you ask St. Joseph about rest and how to incorporate more of it in your life?
3. Ask St. Joseph to pray for you so that you might find deeper rest by trusting in God's providence as deeply as he did.

SECOND WEEK OF ADVENT

WEDNESDAY

Listen: Matthew 1:21

When his mother Mary was betrothed to Joseph, but before they lived together, she was found with child through the holy Spirit. Joseph her husband, since he was a righteous man, yet unwilling to expose her to shame, decided to divorce her quietly. Such was his intention when, behold, the angel of the Lord appeared to him in a dream and said, "Joseph, son of David, do not be afraid to take Mary your wife into your home. For it is through the holy Spirit that this child has been conceived in her. **She will bear a son and you are to name him Jesus, because he will save his people from their sins."** All this took place to fulfill what the Lord had said through the prophet:

"Behold, the virgin shall be with child and
bear a son,
and they shall name him Emmanuel,"

which means "God is with us." When Joseph awoke, he did as the angel of the Lord had commanded him and took his wife into his home. (Mt 1:18–24)

Listen Again

As you begin to meditate on the bolded scripture above, engage your imagination and use the following questions to enter deeply into the scene. What do you imagine it is like for Joseph to find out that he is tasked with naming Jesus? What does he think and feel as he learns from the angel what his role is in God's plan for Mary's child?

Ponder: In and Through

Jesus came to earth during a particularly difficult, violent time in history, a time of severe political corruption and discord. These were far from sanctified times; rather, he came into a world of severe brokenness and sin in order to redeem it.

> Those who are well do not need a physician, but the sick do. I did not come to call the righteous but sinners.
> —Mark 2:17

A difficult, violent time in history with severe political corruption and discord . . . it sounds close to home, doesn't it? Perhaps by coming to first-century Jerusalem with all its political and cultural complications, Jesus wants us to know he can handle the hard things. Perhaps he wants us to know that he doesn't come to us despite difficult, messy situations but rather comes to us *in and through them*.

This is true for each of us personally too. Jesus wants to come all the way into the hardest things in our life. He desires for us to share those things with him. He wants to hear about them from us. Should we dare to let him in—all the way in—he can transform and free us in a way that only God's hand can do.

Respond

1. Is there a specific area of difficulty or "mess" in your life that you have yet to invite Jesus into? What has been holding you back from sharing this part of your life with him?
2. You may have specific prayers and requests of Jesus in the challenging areas of your life—and it is good to share those desires with him. Can you also identify the deeper need you have underneath a specific outcome? Can you name that deeper desire (peace, union, freedom, direction, purpose, etc.)?
3. Ask Jesus to make his presence known to you *in and through* whatever messy situation you are experiencing in your life right now, no matter how big or small it is.

SECOND WEEK OF ADVENT

THURSDAY

Listen: Matthew 1:22–23

When his mother Mary was betrothed to Joseph, but before they lived together, she was found with child through the holy Spirit. Joseph her husband, since he was a righteous man, yet unwilling to expose her to shame, decided to divorce her quietly. Such was his intention when, behold, the angel of the Lord appeared to him in a dream and said, "Joseph, son of David, do not be afraid to take Mary your wife into your home. For it is through the holy Spirit that this child has been conceived in her. She will bear a son and you are to name him Jesus, because he will save his people from their sins." **All this took place to fulfill what the Lord had said through the prophet:**

"Behold, the virgin shall be with child
and bear a son,
and they shall name him Emmanuel,"

which means "God is with us." When Joseph awoke, he did as the angel of the Lord had commanded him and took his wife into his home. (Mt 1:18–24)

Listen Again

As you begin to meditate on the bolded scripture above, engage your imagination and use the following questions to enter deeply into the scene. Joseph was a faithful man who knew the scriptures and prophecies. What was it like for him to hear that they would be fulfilled through Mary, his betrothed? What was it like to understand that he, too, was part of God's plan to fulfill the prophets? How did this reshape his vision of his marriage and life with Mary?

Ponder: Hold My Hand

Recently, during a family gathering when all my siblings and their families were home, I took particular notice of my niece, Lily. She's a feisty, independent little nugget, with an uncanny amount of charm and charisma for a four-year-old. Needless to say, she has me wrapped around her finger.

I was doing something in the kitchen when she excitedly ran over to me, reached up to grab my hand, said, "Hold my hand!" and started leading us to some nook of my parents' house that she wanted to show me. I was struck by how weak her little grip was. To hold her hand, I had to actually *hold on to* her hand. Lily thought she was holding my hand, but in fact, I was very much holding on to hers. She thought that she was with me, but instead, I was very much with her.

And so it is with God.

Our truest and deepest identity is being a son or daughter of God. We are his children, in desperate need of having him hold on to us. My heart melted feeling the gentle grip of Lily's hand trying to hold on to mine. I can't even imagine the delight of God the Father when we reach up—in an act of prayer—to hold his hand. He desires to be with us. He desires to be with *you*, here and now. As much as you think you are reaching toward him as you work through today's reflection and prayer, he is holding on to you even more firmly.

Respond

1. Look back over your life and think of a time when, in hind-sight, you can see that God was present even when you were unaware. How has he directed your life toward good?
2. How is he calling you to abide more deeply in his presence here and now? Do you have any habits or influences that disrupt that sense of union with God?
3. Ask God to help you carry an abiding sense of his presence with you today.

SECOND WEEK OF ADVENT

FRIDAY

Listen: Matthew 1:24

When his mother Mary was betrothed to Joseph, but before they lived together, she was found with child through the holy Spirit. Joseph her husband, since he was a righteous man, yet unwilling to expose her to shame, decided to divorce her quietly. Such was his intention when, behold, the angel of the Lord appeared to him in a dream and said, "Joseph, son of David, do not be afraid to take Mary your wife into your home. For it is through the holy Spirit that this child has been conceived in her. She will bear a son and you are to name him Jesus, because he will save his people from their sins." All this took place to fulfill what the Lord had said through the prophet:

"Behold, the virgin shall be with child and
bear a son,
and they shall name him Emmanuel,"

which means "God is with us." **When Joseph awoke, he did as the angel of the Lord had commanded him and took his wife into his home.** (Mt 1:18–24)

Listen Again

As you begin to meditate on the bolded scripture above, engage your imagination and use the following questions to enter deeply into the scene. Joseph is a righteous and decisive man. What is he feeling and thinking as he wakes with a new understanding and a new decision? What do you think he says to Mary when he sees her next? How does he welcome her into his home? What does his home look like?

Ponder: The Fiat of Joseph

Joseph, in this passage, is giving his own yes, a response of faith that echoes Mary's yes to Gabriel. He is saying yes with complete faith to all that will transpire, both the monotonous moments and the lively ones. By taking Mary into his home, he is saying yes to all that God desires to do. He is giving God the blank check of his entire life and handing over all.

Joseph has much to teach us about humility and hiddenness. Notice that he never speaks in scripture. He seems to appear when it is necessary and then fades once again into the background. But make no mistake, Joseph was the bedrock of the Holy Family. His strength, virtue, and work ethic upheld Mary and Jesus through their lives in Nazareth. In his hiddenness, Joseph was tasked with preparing the Savior of the world for his season of stepping out into public ministry and ultimately the greatest event in human history: Jesus's Death and Resurrection.

My grandpa always used to say that "there's a thrill to monotony." I was young when I heard those words, but the older I get the more I appreciate his poetic wisdom. There really is a beauty and a thrill to the everyday moments of our lives if we have the eyes to see how beautiful they can be.

In a world that encourages us to post everything publicly and try to get as many eyes and likes on our moments of accomplishment, perhaps St. Joseph has something to model for us.

Having community and sharing our lives with one another can be a beautiful thing, but perhaps sometimes it is enough to experience these everyday moments of connection on their own. Perhaps there's a special thrill to holding some of those moments close, not seeking public acknowledgment or affirmation, and seeing what God wants to do with our moments of hiddenness.

Respond

1. How is God inviting you to share some of the moments of your life in a more hidden way with him alone?
2. What is one additional hidden way you might show up for someone in your life this week?
3. Ask St. Joseph to pray for you and help you identify specific ways you can honor your work, your family, and God with quiet, hidden efforts.

SECOND WEEK OF ADVENT

SATURDAY

Return and Recollect

Again, we have an opportunity to pause from our daily rhythm to reflect on what the Lord has done in and for us this week. Think of this as the moment of collecting the gems you have mined this week in prayer and meditation. Instead of laboring ahead, let us pause and return to where we started to fully receive the gift of where we find ourselves today. While this might seem like an unnecessary repetition, be assured that pausing to look back is often when we discover the specific places and patterns in which God has been moving throughout our prayer.

Return and Listen: Matthew 1:18–24

When his mother Mary was betrothed to Joseph, but before they lived together, she was found with child through the holy Spirit. Joseph her husband, since he was a righteous man, yet unwilling to expose her to shame, decided to divorce her quietly. Such was his intention when, behold, the angel of the Lord appeared to him in a dream and said, "Joseph, son of David, do not be afraid to take Mary your wife into your home. For it is through the holy Spirit that this child has been conceived in her. She will bear a son and you are to name him Jesus, because he will save his people from their sins." All this took place to fulfill what the Lord had said through the prophet:

"Behold, the virgin shall be with child and
bear a son,
and they shall name him Emmanuel,"

which means "God is with us." When Joseph awoke, he did as the angel of the Lord had commanded him and took his wife into his home.

Return and Listen Again

Watch the animated video for "Joseph, Righteous Man," which can be found at the link below.

As you encounter the music and artwork again in a more dynamic way, consider how your journey of imaginative prayer through this week has brought this part of the story more to life for you. What has God revealed to you that you had never considered before? What details of the scriptures have come to the surface? What images now exist in your mind's eye when you read these words?

Scan this code with your phone or visit www.avemariapress.com/pages/way-of-the-star-resources **to view the animated art and music from "Joseph, Righteous Man."**

Return and Respond

Collect your prayers from the week by reviewing your journaling notes and writing down anything that stands out to you. As you gather these "gems," pay attention to your own thoughts, feelings, and desires, and write down what you want to remember. Also record here any new observations, continuing questions, or answered prayers that you notice. Take them to Mass with you this evening or tomorrow, and present them on the altar during your Sunday worship. Even as you respond in your journal to everything you have experienced this week, try to remain in a posture of listening for the promptings of the Holy Spirit as you go.

THIRD WEEK OF ADVENT
BETHLEHEM, CITY OF BREAD

THIRD WEEK OF ADVENT

SUNDAY

Listen: Luke 2:1–7

In those days a decree went out from Caesar Augustus that the whole world should be enrolled. . . . So all went to be enrolled, each to his own town. And Joseph too went up from Galilee from the town of Nazareth to Judea, to the city of David that is called Bethlehem, because he was of the house and family of David, to be enrolled with Mary, his betrothed, who was with child. While they were there, the time came for her to have her child, and she gave birth to her firstborn son. She wrapped him in swaddling clothes and laid him in a manger, because there was no room for them in the inn.

Listen Again

Listen to "Bethlehem, City of Bread," which can be found at the link below.

Pay attention to the rhythm, written to mimic the cadence of a donkey's gait, and try to imagine the terrain they are moving over at different points in the song. Imagine the dust and brittle shale underfoot, the hills and scrubby landscape, and the clear sky by day and night. Also, take notice of musical themes and melodies that you heard in previous passages. Try to remember what they signified before and what they might be expressing in the new context of the road to Bethlehem.

While you listen, look at the artwork at the beginning of this chapter and allow your imagination to draw you into the scene. What do you imagine Mary and Joseph doing as they journey together on the road to Bethlehem? What do they talk about? Laugh about? Express concern about? Do they pray together? Do they pray for each other in the silence of their own hearts? What is weighing most on Joseph's mind as he leads Mary, who is with child? What is Mary pondering most deeply in her heart? How does this journey prepare them for the birth of their son, Jesus?

Scan this code with your phone or visit www.avemariapress.com/pages/way-of-the-star-resources to find a video introduction to this week's prayer themes and a recording of "Bethlehem, City of Bread."

Ponder: Slow and Steady

For this third week of Advent, we journey to Bethlehem with the Holy Family. With the roads as they existed then, the journey from Nazareth to Bethlehem would have been a trip of eighty or ninety miles. Mary, being far along in her pregnancy, needed a means of travel that would allow as much comfort as possible.

Tortoises are famously known for their "slow and steady wins the race" motto, but it's possible they have a decent contender for that title in donkeys. Donkeys are just that: slow but very steady. While they were much slower than other animals used for transportation, they were able to walk long distances, especially on difficult terrain, with a fair amount of ease. Joseph and Mary could travel only by daylight and probably had to take breaks during the day, considering Mary's condition. Barring weather, they most likely traveled six or eight hours per day, at a very modest pace. Donkeys were chosen for safety and consistency, not for speed.

We are halfway through Advent—it is Gaudete Sunday! *Gaudete* is a Latin term that means "rejoice." We rejoice because our celebration of the feast of the Savior's birth is nearly here, and there is much reason to hope.

As we shared at the beginning of this journey, this Way of the Star is unlike any other Advent you have experienced before, and it will be unlike any Advent you will experience again. Grace is never recycled. God is leading the way and making all things new. He knows perfectly the destination where he desires you to arrive and the timing it will take to get you there. If your progress feels slow or even stagnant, remember that God chose the vehicle for Joseph, Mary, and Jesus, and they arrived at Bethlehem exactly when he intended them to.

Respond

1. Here at the halfway mark of our Advent journey, take a moment to review the progress you've made in prayer. How has this experience of imaginative prayer through scripture, music, and art been for you? In what ways do you see God

inviting you to embrace patience and trust in the progress you are making this Advent?

2. What practices or habits help you stay grounded in a "slow and steady" approach to this season? In the midst of all the to-do lists and plans that you face each day, what daily habit can you introduce to recenter yourself in God's peaceful presence?
3. Ask Mary and Joseph to intercede for any specific areas of struggle with pace or timing you're experiencing, either in your everyday life or interior life, at this point in your Advent journey.

THIRD WEEK OF ADVENT

MONDAY

Listen: Luke 2:1–3

In those days a decree went out from Caesar Augustus that the whole world should be enrolled. . . . So all went to be enrolled, each to his own town. And Joseph too went up from Galilee from the town of Nazareth to Judea, to the city of David that is called Bethlehem, because he was of the house and family of David, to be enrolled with Mary, his betrothed, who was with child. While they were there, the time came for her to have her child, and she gave birth to her firstborn son. She wrapped him in swaddling clothes and laid him in a manger, because there was no room for them in the inn. (Lk 2:1–7)

Listen Again

As you begin to meditate on the bolded scripture above, engage your imagination and use the following questions to enter deeply into the scene. Who announces the news of the census in Nazareth? How do Mary and Joseph receive the news of all it will require of them? How does this affect the months of planning and preparation that Joseph and Mary have made for the birth of their son? What is the general feeling in Nazareth as all are forced to travel to another place to fulfill the census?

Ponder: Live Interrupted

I have a friend who has adopted for her life an intriguing mantra: "Live interrupted." In a culture that is scheduled minute to minute, with symphonies of alarms and notifications telling us where to be and when, sometimes the most amazing things happen when we are unexpectedly interrupted and the course of our day is redirected. The majority of Jesus's recorded miracles in the gospels, in fact, happened when he was on his way to somewhere else. With his heart and mind moving in one direction, he was suddenly interrupted, and his openness to these unexpected encounters resulted in miracles. His willingness to be interrupted is a beautiful lesson for us.

But let's not idealize this lesson too much—being interrupted sometimes comes with another experience: the inconvenience of changing our plans. From the very start, the Holy Family was formed around inconvenience. The angel Gabriel did not bring convenient messages to Mary or Joseph. Jesus's message of Good News was anything but convenient for anyone who heard it. Sometimes the most miraculous and beautiful experiences in our lives come after being interrupted, that is, if we are open to those interruptions and allow God to redirect us as he sees fit. And therein lies good discernment: Am I being asked to forge ahead and be steadfast, or am I being asked to yield to another way? The only way to know is by learning to recognize the voice and movement of God in a living relationship that is cultivated and strengthened by meeting him daily in prayer.

Respond

1. In what ways do you perceive God interrupting your life during this season of Advent or this season of your life? In what ways is he inviting you to respond?
2. What inconveniences have you welcomed to cultivate your relationship with him? What further inconveniences might God be inviting you to consider?
3. Spend time praying for wisdom and good discernment to recognize God's voice more clearly.

THIRD WEEK OF ADVENT

TUESDAY

Listen: Luke 2:4

In those days a decree went out from Caesar Augustus that the whole world should be enrolled. . . . So all went to be enrolled, each to his own town. **And Joseph too went up from Galilee from the town of Nazareth to Judea, to the city of David that is called Bethlehem,** because he was of the house and family of David, to be enrolled with Mary, his betrothed, who was with child. While they were there, the time came for her to have her child, and she gave birth to her firstborn son. She wrapped him in swaddling clothes and laid him in a manger, because there was no room for them in the inn. (Lk 2:1–7)

Listen Again

As you begin to meditate on the bolded scripture above, engage your imagination and use the following questions to enter deeply into the scene. What is the disposition of Joseph and Mary's hearts as they set out on their journey to Bethlehem? How do you think they prepared for their journey? What do they pack, and what do they leave behind? What does the road look like? What is the weather like? Do they travel alone, or do others join them on the journey?

Ponder: House of Bread

"And you, Bethlehem, land of Judah, are by no means least among the rulers of Judah; since from you shall come a ruler, who is to shepherd my people Israel" (Mt 2:6). Matthew is quoting Micah 5:1, which recalls Bethlehem as the birthplace of the great King David and foretold it as the place of an even greater ruler.

Bethlehem comes from the Hebrew words *beit* and *lechem*, which together mean "house of bread." This is a prophetic foreshadowing that from the city of Bethlehem—the house of bread—would come the One who is the Bread of Life for the world. What divine poetry! Both Micah and Matthew highlight a consistent theme that reappears throughout the story of salvation history: God uses humble, ordinary instruments and places to accomplish his glorious will. These references call to mind the Last Supper, when Jesus identifies himself as the unleavened bread that he takes, blesses, breaks, and shares with his disciples. Of every possible element on planet earth, he chooses the most common household material as the means with which to give us his very Body, in which we find nourishment and new life.

In a simple loaf of bread and in the small town of Bethlehem, we see what wonders God can work in and through very humble things. He will do no less with whatever humble space we can offer him as a dwelling place in our hearts.

Respond

1. Recall a specific moment when you experienced the Eucharist as an extraordinary gift. Why did it move you? What aspects of the experience were humble, and how did you experience it as exalted?
2. When have you seen moments or situations in your life that seemed humble and unworthy turn into extraordinary encounters with God or others? What practices or habits can open your awareness to God's presence in your everyday experience?
3. Give thanks to Jesus for sustaining and nourishing us with his presence in the Eucharist, and ask him how you might embody his love in the situations you will face today.

THIRD WEEK OF ADVENT

WEDNESDAY

Listen: Luke 2:4–5

In those days a decree went out from Caesar Augustus that the whole world should be enrolled. . . . So all went to be enrolled, each to his own town. And Joseph too went up from Galilee from the town of Nazareth to Judea, to the city of David that is called Bethlehem, **because he was of the house and family of David, to be enrolled with Mary, his betrothed, who was with child.** While they were there, the time came for her to have her child, and she gave birth to her firstborn son. She wrapped him in swaddling clothes and laid him in a manger, because there was no room for them in the inn. (Lk 2:1–7)

Listen Again

As you begin to meditate on the bolded scripture above, engage your imagination and use the following questions to enter deeply into the scene. As they walk the road to Bethlehem, does Mary ask Joseph to tell her stories about his royal ancestral heritage? What kind of reflections do they share about how God is quietly bringing about the fulfillment of his prophecies through their child? What questions do they have? What is their posture toward one another as they talk and pray together? What gives them the strength to renew their yes to God's plan?

Ponder: Hidden in Plain Sight

Jesus didn't appear among us as a developed adult, though he very well could have. He came instead as a helpless baby who needed to grow and learn as we all do. More accurately, though, Jesus *first* came to us as an embryo.

He chose to be hidden for nine months in Mary's womb before anybody could see him. He was again hidden for thirty years before stepping into the public eye. The God of the universe chose to be hidden in plain sight for the majority of his life, allowing much of his earthly time to be spent in small, hidden ways that largely didn't make it into the four gospel accounts.

In my own life, I have started to discover how much God loves process. He literally spoke life into being. In Genesis, he says a word and it comes to be—just like that, immediately. But not so with Jesus becoming man. He chose a different way. There are absolutely moments when God moves quickly and the results are immediate (and praise God when we get to experience those interventions). But perhaps he also wants us to know there is great beauty and power in the situations in our lives, especially the hidden ones, that take a little—or a lot—more time.

Respond

1. Most of our life unfolds in hidden and humble ways. How have you experienced God at work in these quiet moments over this season of Advent? Make a list of how God has made his presence known to you.
2. Mary and Joseph had to attend to the new life growing in their family even when no one else knew what was happening—Mary's pregnancy meant radically reorienting their lives to make room for Jesus. What is one way God is calling you to reorient your life to grow and sustain your relationship with him?
3. Ask Mary and Joseph to pray for you so that you can grow more attentive to the hidden ways God is at work in your life and will have the courage to respond to what he is inviting you to.

THIRD WEEK OF ADVENT

THURSDAY

Listen: Luke 2:6–7

In those days a decree went out from Caesar Augustus that the whole world should be enrolled. . . . So all went to be enrolled, each to his own town. And Joseph too went up from Galilee from the town of Nazareth to Judea, to the city of David that is called Bethlehem, because he was of the house and family of David, to be enrolled with Mary, his betrothed, who was with child. **While they were there, the time came for her to have her child, and she gave birth to her firstborn son.** She wrapped him in swaddling clothes and laid him in a manger, because there was no room for them in the inn. (Lk 2:1–7)

Listen Again

As you begin to meditate on the bolded scripture above, engage your imagination and use the following questions to enter deeply into the scene. How and where do you imagine Mary and Joseph expected their son to be born? How different from that expectation is the situation they find themselves in? As Mary begins to feel the first signs of labor, what feelings do you think they experience as they are still looking for a place to stay the night? How do you imagine them praying for God to provide for them? What is it like for them to find shelter in the stable?

Ponder: Off the Christmas Card

I am no expert on stables, but the few I have ever walked into in my life have immediately flooded my senses—I had no choice but to take in the robust smells, sights, sounds, and textures all around me. The smells from the many animals that occupy the space are less than pleasant. The breathing, *moo*-ing, snorting, *bah*-ing, and rustling of the field animals settling into stalls echo almost in a duet with the wind whistling through the cracks in the thin wooden walls of the stable itself. It seems as though everything I can smell, I can also taste—it's just in the air. It's difficult to know where to sit down in a stable, as they are not built for human visitors or social interaction. Put plainly, stables can be very dirty and uncomfortable. They're definitely not optimal places for a newborn baby or a new mother.

But then we look a little bit deeper. To consider the reality of Jesus's birth opens our imaginations and expands our expectations for how we think God works in our lives. Joseph and Mary, in their persistent faithfulness, trusted God in what looked like impossible circumstances. He did not lead them to a hospital or palace, but he did meet their needs—and he did so in a way that let his glory shine through everyday, ordinary elements.

A dear spiritual confidant once invited me to reflect on the scene of the birth of Christ. With her invitation came a piece of advice: "Take the manger scene off the Christmas card." What she meant was that in the beautiful decor, lighted trees, and even well-planned Christmas pageants and parties, it is tempting to romanticize this story. This was not glamorous in any way. This was very, very hard.

It is undeniable that fruit can come from suffering. God could have spared Mary and Joseph the discomfort of this experience, but he allowed it—and walked with them through it. And because Mary and Joseph were in a place like a stable, a group of less-than-presentable shepherds were able to arrive unannounced and spend time with the baby King. Jesus came to bring Good News, and from his very first moment, God was drawing everyone—especially those on the margins—toward him. Mary and Joseph couldn't see those implications when they were searching for a place to stay, but they continued to trust God.

No matter what state we are in—physical, spiritual, or otherwise—Jesus wants us to come to him. The challenging and difficult circumstances of his birth reveal that there is no place he would not go to reach us.

Respond

1. When you "take the manger scene off the Christmas card," what new reality—the difficulty and the beauty—do you see in how God allowed the birth of his Son to come about?
2. What parts of your life feel dirty, messy, or dysfunctional? Name them specifically.
3. In your prayer today, invite Jesus into these messy areas. If that feels too difficult, ask him for the grace to help you invite him into your life more fully.

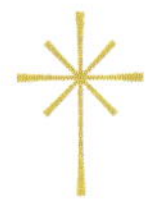

THIRD WEEK OF ADVENT

FRIDAY

Listen: Luke 2:7

In those days a decree went out from Caesar Augustus that the whole world should be enrolled. . . . So all went to be enrolled, each to his own town. And Joseph too went up from Galilee from the town of Nazareth to Judea, to the city of David that is called Bethlehem, because he was of the house and family of David, to be enrolled with Mary, his betrothed, who was with child. While they were there, the time came for her to have her child, and she gave birth to her firstborn son. **She wrapped him in swaddling clothes and laid him in a manger, because there was no room for them in the inn.** (Lk 2:1–7)

Listen Again

As you begin to meditate on the bolded scripture above, engage your imagination and use the following questions to enter deeply into the scene. Imagine watching Mary carefully wrapping her newborn son in the swaddling clothes. What do Mary and Joseph experience as they hold Jesus in their arms for the first time? How do they encounter God in him? What is it like for them to welcome the Savior of the world into their family as an infant they hold in the rugged simplicity of a stable?

> The stone the builders rejected
> has become the cornerstone.
> —Psalm 118:22

Ponder: Prepare Him Room

As Jesus rode into Bethlehem in Mary's womb, the Holy Family met hearts and minds that refused to make room for them. Many years later, Jesus would ride into Jerusalem in triumph before suffering and dying at the hands of those who would not accept him as King—they, too, were unwilling to prepare room for him. Still today, there are moments when we, too, deny him room—in our communities, in our families, and in our own hearts. And in his complete respect of our free will, he will never barge his way in.

Respond

1. With the guidance of the Holy Spirit, identify any specific ways you have rejected Jesus or failed to make room for him. What do you want to say to Jesus about those places? Listen to what he wants to say to you.
2. We know that Jesus is present "in the least of these" (Mt 25:40). What is a specific opportunity your parish, community,

neighborhood, or family has to welcome or serve someone in need this Advent season?

3. Ask the Holy Spirit for deeper and more courageous faithfulness to act on that opportunity.

THIRD WEEK OF ADVENT

SATURDAY

Return and Recollect

Again, we have an opportunity to pause from our daily rhythm to reflect on what the Lord has done in and for us this week. Think of this as the moment of collecting the gems you have mined this week in prayer and meditation. Instead of laboring ahead, let us pause and return to where we started to fully receive the gift of where we find ourselves today. While this might seem like an unnecessary repetition, be assured that pausing to look back is often when we discover the specific places and patterns in which God has been moving throughout our prayer.

Return and Listen: Luke 2:1–7

In those days a decree went out from Caesar Augustus that the whole world should be enrolled. . . . So all went to be enrolled, each to his own town. And Joseph too went up from Galilee from the town of Nazareth to Judea, to the city of David that is called Bethlehem, because he was of the house and family of David, to be enrolled with Mary, his betrothed, who was with child. While they were there, the time came for her to have her child, and she gave birth to her firstborn son. She wrapped him in swaddling clothes and laid him in a manger, because there was no room for them in the inn.

Return and Listen Again

Watch the animated video for "Bethlehem, City of Bread," which can be found at the link below.

As you encounter the music and artwork again in a more dynamic way, consider how your journey of imaginative prayer through this week has brought this part of the story more to life for you. What has God revealed to you that you had never considered before? What details of the scriptures have come to the surface? What images now exist in your mind's eye when you read these words?

Scan this code with your phone or visit www.avemariapress.com/pages/way-of-the-star-resources to view animated art and music for "Bethlehem, City of Bread."

Return and Respond

Collect your prayers from the week by reviewing your journaling notes and writing down anything that stands out to you. As you gather these "gems," pay attention to your own thoughts, feelings, and desires, and write down what you want to remember. Also record here any new observations, continuing questions, or answered prayers that you notice. Take them to Mass with you this evening or tomorrow, and present them on the altar during your Sunday worship. Even as you respond in your journal to everything you have experienced this week, try to remain in a posture of listening for the promptings of the Holy Spirit as you go.

FOURTH WEEK OF ADVENT

SHEPHERDS, KEEPING WATCH

FOURTH WEEK OF ADVENT

SUNDAY

Listen: Luke 2:8–20

Now there were shepherds in that region living in the fields and keeping the night watch over their flock. The angel of the Lord appeared to them and the glory of the Lord shone around them, and they were struck with great fear. The angel said to them, "Do not be afraid; for behold, I proclaim to you good news of great joy that will be for all the people. For today in the city of David a savior has been born for you who is Messiah and Lord. And this will be a sign for you: you will find an infant wrapped in swaddling clothes and lying in a manger." And suddenly there was a multitude of the heavenly host with the angel, praising God and saying:

> "Glory to God in the highest
> and on earth peace to those on whom his
> favor rests."

When the angels went away from them to heaven, the shepherds said to one another, "Let us go, then, to Bethlehem to see this thing that has taken place, which the Lord has made known to us." So they went in haste and found Mary and Joseph, and the infant lying in the manger. When they saw this, they made known the message that had been told them about this child.

All who heard it were amazed by what had been told them by the shepherds. And Mary kept all these things, reflecting on them in her heart. Then the shepherds returned, glorifying and praising God for all they had heard and seen, just as it had been told to them.

Listen Again

Listen to "Shepherds, Keeping Watch," which can be found at the link on the next page.

Pay attention to any new instrumentation that you hear at the beginning of the song, and imagine how this signifies the way the shepherds would sing or play simple instruments to calm and call their flocks. Imagine the shepherds' music drifting over the fields beneath the night sky. Listen as the tempo quickens and the fanfare begins, indicating the appearance and announcement of the angel and heavenly hosts. Notice how the music of the heavens does not overtake the music of the shepherds but rather interacts with it, revealing this moment of convergence between the heavens and the earth.

While you listen, look at the artwork at the beginning of this chapter and allow your imagination to draw you into the scene. What do you imagine the shepherds doing just before the angel appears? Are they keeping warm around a fire? Singing a psalm from their ancestor David, who used to keep watch in the same fields? What do they see at the angel's appearance that makes them afraid? What does it sound like when they hear the multitude of the heavenly hosts singing praise to God? What do they say to one another when the angels depart? Imagine them recounting to one another what they have seen and heard. Do they believe this message? Would you? How do they find Mary and Joseph? How do they greet them when they see them? What do Mary and Joseph think of the story the shepherds share with them?

Scan this code with your phone or visit www.avemariapress.com/pages/way-of-the-star-resources to find a video introduction to this week's prayer themes and a recording of "Shepherds, Keeping Watch."

Ponder: A Lesson from Our Lady of Sorrows

Before attending a silent retreat, I had never really prayed with my imagination before, nor had I ever attempted to place myself into a scripture story. But there I was at a beautiful retreat center on the coast of Tampa Bay, diving into a prompt to reflect on the passion of Jesus and try to place myself in the story.

I remember closing my eyes, trying to picture Calvary. Immediately, in my imagination, I could see the scene of the Pietà, with Mary on the ground holding Jesus's body. In my imagination, I was a spectator to this scene, keeping my distance—again, I was very new to this type of prayer. Suddenly, I imagined Mary looking up—she was looking right at me. I was a little startled. She had nothing but love in her eyes, and she motioned for me to come closer. I looked around, thinking, "Is she pointing to me?" She lovingly met my gaze and nodded. I walked over to her, feeling very unworthy to be in this sacred moment with Mary and Jesus.

What she did next was really astounding to me. She snapped off one of the thorns from the crown on Jesus's head, opened my hand, and gently placed it in my palm, using her hand to close my fingers over it. There was a silent exchange in prayer I won't attempt to describe here, but when I turned to walk away, I opened my hand . . . to find that the thorn had turned to pure gold. When I opened my eyes from this prayer experience, I was stunned to find that unbeknownst to me, I was sitting in the middle of a rose garden, full of thorns, with a statue of the Pietà right next to me. A God of details!

I have thought of that moment many times since. In retrospect, Mary did for me in that moment what she does for all of humanity at every moment, and it's the same thing that she did in the stable at Bethlehem: She invites us to come closer to her son and to receive the gifts he has to offer, especially in moments of suffering when we feel as if we are alone or unworthy. In that mysterious exchange, I think she was showing me that even the greatest sufferings of our lives the Lord can turn into great glory.

> We know that all things work for good for those who love God, who are called according to his purpose.
> —Romans 8:28

Respond

1. What kinds of suffering or "thorns" is God allowing you to experience right now? In what ways might God be refining you or your family through this particular suffering?
2. Imagine Mary receiving the shepherds who came to worship her son. In what ways is Mary inviting you to come closer to Jesus?
3. Ask Mary—Our Lady of Sorrows—to help you see how God is working the circumstances of your life to the good right now, especially the areas of hardship and suffering.

FOURTH WEEK OF ADVENT

MONDAY

Listen: Luke 2:8–10

Now there were shepherds in that region living in the fields and keeping the night watch over their flock. The angel of the Lord appeared to them and the glory of the Lord shone around them, and they were struck with great fear. The angel said to them, "Do not be afraid; for behold, I proclaim to you good news of great joy that will be for all the people. For today in the city of David a savior has been born for you who is Messiah and Lord. And this will be a sign for you: you will find an infant wrapped in swaddling clothes and lying in a manger." And suddenly there was a multitude of the heavenly host with the angel, praising God and saying:

"Glory to God in the highest
and on earth peace to those on whom his
favor rests."

When the angels went away from them to heaven, the shepherds said to one another, "Let us go, then, to Bethlehem to see this thing that has taken place, which the Lord has made known to us." So they went in haste and found Mary and Joseph, and the infant lying in the manger. When they saw this, they made known the message that had been told them about this child. All who heard it were amazed by what had been told them by the shepherds. And Mary kept all these things, reflecting on them in her heart. Then the shepherds returned, glorifying and praising God for all they had heard and seen, just as it had been told to them. (Lk 2:8–20)

Listen Again

As you begin to meditate on the bolded scripture above, engage your imagination and use the following questions to enter deeply into the scene. Imagine the fields where the shepherds keep watch—what do they look like? How many shepherds are there? What do they see as the glory of the Lord shines all around them? What kind of fear are they struck with? What does it sound like when the angel speaks to them, and how does this affect their fear?

Ponder: And the Last Shall Be First

As we have started to explore already throughout this Advent season, it is undeniable that throughout scripture God routinely chooses lowly, unlikely candidates to accomplish great things for him. Before anyone else on the entire planet heard this good news, the Holy Spirit chose to announce the birth of Jesus Christ to shepherds who were essentially doing a humble night shift. And by virtue of being the first to receive this good news, they are also the first human beings to have the opportunity to announce the birth of Christ to the rest of the world. Pretty amazing.

Shepherds were historically a rough band of brothers—they were not known for astute academics, nor were they typically people of great affluence. They lived much of their lives outside, dealing with the natural elements and animals and handling a myriad of potential threats to the sheep they tended. They sat on the outskirts of civilized society back then—a marginalized group.

That being said, there is also a quality that shepherds strongly possessed that causes me to wonder if it is perhaps why God chose them to first receive the news of Christ's birth: They were watchful and vigilant. Linguistically, *vigilance* is a term directly connected to keeping watch and praying outside of normal hours, particularly in the late evening—think of a vigil. Put simply, the shepherds were awake when nobody else was. And God can do a lot with someone who is awake and paying attention.

Respond

1. In this final week of Advent, how is God inviting you to be alert? What are some practical ways in which you sense God is inviting you to be more aware and vigilant in hearing his voice?
2. Who are people around you who need to hear the Good News of God's love for them? How could you proclaim it to them?
3. Ask your guardian angel to help you be awake and vigilant to the Good News God wants to proclaim in your life and the Good News he is calling you to proclaim to others.

FOURTH WEEK OF ADVENT

TUESDAY

Listen: Luke 2:11–12

Now there were shepherds in that region living in the fields and keeping the night watch over their flock. The angel of the Lord appeared to them and the glory of the Lord shone around them, and they were struck with great fear. The angel said to them, "Do not be afraid; for behold, I proclaim to you good news of great joy that will be for all the people. **For today in the city of David a savior has been born for you who is Messiah and Lord. And this will be a sign for you: you will find an infant wrapped in swaddling clothes and lying in a manger."** And suddenly there was a multitude of the heavenly host with the angel, praising God and saying:

"Glory to God in the highest
and on earth peace to those on whom his
favor rests."

When the angels went away from them to heaven, the shepherds said to one another, "Let us go, then, to Bethlehem to see this thing that has taken place, which the Lord has made known to us." So they went in haste and found Mary and Joseph, and the infant lying in the manger. When they saw this, they made known the message that had been told them about

this child. All who heard it were amazed by what had been told them by the shepherds. And Mary kept all these things, reflecting on them in her heart. Then the shepherds returned, glorifying and praising God for all they had heard and seen, just as it had been told to them. (Lk 2:8–20)

Listen Again

As you begin to meditate on the bolded scripture above, engage your imagination and use the following questions to enter deeply into the scene. When the shepherds hear the angel say the word *Messiah*, what feeling is raised in their hearts? What expectations take shape in their minds at this news? How do you think they responded to the humble sign of an infant wrapped in swaddling clothes?

Ponder: A God of Details

I want to invite you to think of your favorite piece of art. It can be a song, a painting, a piece of architecture, a play, a book, or a film. Pause for one minute and bring a specific piece of art to mind. Take your time.

Whatever piece of art you are now thinking of—along with every other beautiful piece of art in the world that is and ever was—has been inspired by a single Source.

Such beauty feels so unnecessary, so gratuitous. God deeply cares about beautiful things, and in his kindness, he has fashioned our hearts for beauty. This is the reason a gorgeous sunset stops us in our tracks. It is why you are drawn to whatever piece of artwork you chose a moment ago. God chooses beauty as one of the means he uses to communicate to us. He loves the grandeur of a sunset in the sky or the Sistine Chapel just as much as the smallest feature on a mustard seed or the subtlest of musical motifs. He is a God of great detail and the ultimate Artist.

"You will find an infant wrapped in swaddling clothes and lying in a manger." Of everything the angel said to the shepherds, this seems like such a small, specific detail to include. Perhaps this detail was something for them to hold on to in a moment when they were overwhelmed or even doubtful of what they had just experienced. A swaddled baby lying in a manger would have been a very unlikely thing for them to find, so this detail would confirm in their minds what they were looking for and assure them when they found him.

Sometimes during the homestretch of Advent, I am tempted to check out of Advent mode and step into the excitement of Christmas. Practically speaking, there is much to prepare, and it is difficult to remain still and attentive. But grace is available to us only in the present moment. We can receive Advent graces only during Advent. God has more he wants to give you.

Respond

1. In these final days of Advent, which details, large or small, of Jesus's infancy narrative stick out to you? What portions of the story do you feel drawn to? Are there any themes—maybe unexpected ones—that have come up in your prayer throughout this season?
2. Create space in your prayer today to ask the Lord about the details of his story that stay with you. Be curious. Enter into dialogue with him. Why those themes and details? Is there something he wants to show you?
3. Ask God to help you notice and respond to someone in your life with loving attention to detail.

FOURTH WEEK OF ADVENT

WEDNESDAY

Listen: Luke 2:13–14

Now there were shepherds in that region living in the fields and keeping the night watch over their flock. The angel of the Lord appeared to them and the glory of the Lord shone around them, and they were struck with great fear. The angel said to them, "Do not be afraid; for behold, I proclaim to you good news of great joy that will be for all the people. For today in the city of David a savior has been born for you who is Messiah and Lord. And this will be a sign for you: you will find an infant wrapped in swaddling clothes and lying in a manger." **And suddenly there was a multitude of the heavenly host with the angel, praising God and saying:**

> **"Glory to God in the highest**
> **and on earth peace to those on whom**
> **his favor rests."**

When the angels went away from them to heaven, the shepherds said to one another, "Let us go, then, to Bethlehem to see this thing that has taken place, which the Lord has made known to us." So they went in haste and found Mary and Joseph, and the infant lying in the manger. When they saw this, they made known the message that had been told them about

this child. All who heard it were amazed by what had been told them by the shepherds. And Mary kept all these things, reflecting on them in her heart. Then the shepherds returned, glorifying and praising God for all they had heard and seen, just as it had been told to them. (Lk 2:8–20)

Listen Again

As you begin to meditate on the bolded scripture above, engage your imagination and use the following questions to enter deeply into the scene. As the vision changes and the heavenly hosts sing the glory of God, what do the shepherds hear and see? How are they overwhelmed by the heavenly beauty they encounter—what feelings do they experience? If they were to try to describe this moment to you, what would they say?

Ponder: And Suddenly

The ancient Celts used to call the Holy Spirit the "Wild Goose." If you have yet to experience watching the movement of wild geese, I highly recommend a quick internet search. Wild geese are just that: unpredictable. One moment they are docile and calm, and the next they are walking quickly while flapping spastically with their wide wingspan.

One moment the skies are quiet in Bethlehem, and the next they are filled with light and sound as celestial beings sent by the Holy Spirit announce the birth of Christ. The Wild Goose, indeed. Can you imagine what that was like for the shepherds to experience that? The darkness of the sky suddenly illuminated with heavenly light! Life with the Holy Spirit—should we decide to let the Spirit guide our lives—truly is the greatest of adventures. The Spirit's movement in our lives can happen subtly and slowly, or it can be obvious and sudden, as it was in Bethlehem that night. Scripture speaks quite a bit about God's timing and waiting on it. At the core of waiting on the Lord is the reality that he is in control and deciding when and how things happen, not us.

Instant gratification has been progressively sewn into the fabric of our society, and it has no doubt affected the way I wait and how long I'm willing to be patient. I can grab my phone and have groceries delivered to my front door within an hour. And while the temptation to want things to happen quickly definitely needs to be tempered, it isn't to be demonized entirely. God shows us in this scripture passage that sometimes he loves—and opts for—things to happen suddenly.

My mom has told us over the years that *we can't see what God sees*. It's important for us to remember that God's ways are higher than ours, and whether we're being asked to wait or if God is acting suddenly in our lives, our response actually ought to be the same regardless: trust and confidence in him.

Respond

1. God's movement in our lives tends to be consistent. What are some ways you have seen God move in your life, both slowly over time and also suddenly?
2. Does anything get in the way of your responsiveness to the new and surprising things God brings you to? What causes the hesitation?
3. Ask God for greater trust and confidence in him, regardless of the pace things seem to be moving in your life right now.

FOURTH WEEK OF ADVENT

THURSDAY

Listen: Luke 2:15–16

Now there were shepherds in that region living in the fields and keeping the night watch over their flock. The angel of the Lord appeared to them and the glory of the Lord shone around them, and they were struck with great fear. The angel said to them, "Do not be afraid; for behold, I proclaim to you good news of great joy that will be for all the people. For today in the city of David a savior has been born for you who is Messiah and Lord. And this will be a sign for you: you will find an infant wrapped in swaddling clothes and lying in a manger." And suddenly there was a multitude of the heavenly host with the angel, praising God and saying:

> "Glory to God in the highest
> and on earth peace to those on whom his
> favor rests."

When the angels went away from them to heaven, the shepherds said to one another, "Let us go, then, to Bethlehem to see this thing that has taken place, which the Lord has made known to us." So they went in haste and found Mary and Joseph, and the infant lying in the manger. When they saw this, they made known the message that had been told them about

this child. All who heard it were amazed by what had been told them by the shepherds. And Mary kept all these things, reflecting on them in her heart. Then the shepherds returned, glorifying and praising God for all they had heard and seen, just as it had been told to them. (Lk 2:8–20)

Listen Again

As you begin to meditate on the bolded scripture above, engage your imagination and use the following questions to enter deeply into the scene. Imagine yourself in the field with the shepherds as the angels return to heaven. Who is the first shepherd to speak—what does he say? What is their conversation like in that moment? As they make their way to Bethlehem, how do they look for and find Jesus, Mary, and Joseph? What do they experience as they behold the faces of Jesus and his parents?

Ponder: In Haste

One Saturday, I remember having a sudden, pressing feeling that I should go to Confession. I didn't know why, but I had a pretty strong sense that I should promptly drop what I was doing, get in my car, and go.

I had recently been at a function at the university where I was working at the time, and met the wife of a professor I had when I was a student. As I stood in line for Confession that Saturday afternoon, I saw her come out of the confessional. I watched as she slowly went into one of the pews close to me and reached down for the kneeler to offer her penance. But as she reached to pull down the kneeler, she completely collapsed. I immediately ran over to her, unsure if she was conscious. Her legs were still in the pew, and her upper torso was strewn in the aisle. Addressing her by name, I remember saying, "Hi, my name is Andrea. I met you with your husband just the other week. I'm here! Can you hear me?"

"Yes," she said calmly. "I think I'm having a stroke." She was unable to move—her right side was limp. I motioned for some of the young men in line for Confession to come over and help lift her more comfortably into the aisle. As we waited for the ambulance, I simply stayed and waited with her. I'm sure she was terrified, and I wanted to make sure she knew she was not alone.

After a short time at the hospital following her stroke, this dear woman passed away. I was stunned and very sad to hear the news. Sometime after her funeral, her husband called me and, with great emotion in his voice, shared with me that he was initially told that she was on her way into Confession when she collapsed. But someone told him that I was there and could attest that she was actually coming out of the confessional. He told me that was the greatest gift he could have received, knowing that his beloved wife had just received the Sacrament of Reconciliation before going to meet her Lord.

When God prompts us to do something in haste, we must go *in haste*. The shepherds "went in haste" to search for Jesus immediately after the angels' greeting. We must have the same urgency in responding to the Spirit. We do not always know why, but our prompt obedience greatly matters, both here and in the eyes of eternity.

Respond

1. Is there anything in your life, internal or external, that God is asking you to address with haste?
2. The shepherds had clarity about the message they received and acted promptly. What is the message God has been speaking to you this Advent? How can you respond to it with urgency?

3. Ask God to grant you clarity and urgency in responding to his will for your life.

FOURTH WEEK OF ADVENT

FRIDAY

Listen: Luke 2:17–20

Now there were shepherds in that region living in the fields and keeping the night watch over their flock. The angel of the Lord appeared to them and the glory of the Lord shone around them, and they were struck with great fear. The angel said to them, "Do not be afraid; for behold, I proclaim to you good news of great joy that will be for all the people. For today in the city of David a savior has been born for you who is Messiah and Lord. And this will be a sign for you: you will find an infant wrapped in swaddling clothes and lying in a manger." And suddenly there was a multitude of the heavenly host with the angel, praising God and saying:

> "Glory to God in the highest
> and on earth peace to those on whom his
> favor rests."

When the angels went away from them to heaven, the shepherds said to one another, "Let us go, then, to Bethlehem to see this thing that has taken place, which the Lord has made known to us." So they went in haste and found Mary and Joseph, and the infant lying in the manger. **When they saw this, they made known the message that had been told them about**

this child. All who heard it were amazed by what had been told them by the shepherds. And Mary kept all these things, reflecting on them in her heart. Then the shepherds returned, glorifying and praising God for all they had heard and seen, just as it had been told to them. (Lk 2:8–20)

Listen Again

As you begin to meditate on the bolded scripture above, engage your imagination and use the following questions to enter deeply into the scene. Imagine yourself standing in the place where Mary and Joseph are with Jesus as the shepherds arrive and enter. As they tell Mary and Joseph about the vision they saw in the fields and the message the angel spoke to them, how do Mary and Joseph respond? Do they in turn tell the shepherds about the appearances of the angel Gabriel that they experienced? As Mary reflects on all these things in her heart, what thoughts and emotions stir in her? As Mary places Jesus in the arms of each shepherd to hold, what do they experience?

Ponder: The Secret Place

A spiritual mentor of mine once said to me, "Sometimes we are supposed to go in haste, and other times we're supposed to ponder things in our hearts as Mary did. The difference lies in good discernment of what God is asking of us at any given moment." I think of her words as we spend back-to-back days reflecting on the shepherds going in haste and Mary pondering in stillness the many things that she experienced.

There is great power in being a person of action. But the action in our lives becomes efficacious only when the source and guide of that power is God—otherwise we are simply busy and hectic. We learn how to be with God in stillness and hear his voice when we go, as scripture tells us, to the secret place: "But when you pray, go to your inner room, close the door, and pray to your Father in secret. And your Father who sees in secret will repay you" (Mt 6:6).

Mary understood this and is the model par excellence of remaining ever close to the Source. In his book *The Power of Silence: Against the Dictatorship of Noise*, Cardinal Robert Sarah echoes this truth when he writes that "prayer consists of listening to God speak silently within us."

Pondering is different from merely thinking about or analyzing something, and it is also not reduced to only feelings. Pondering engages both the mind and the heart. As Cardinal Sarah reminds us, prayer consists of listening to God speaking within us and paying close attention to the movements of our mind and heart. As a musician, I love the analogy of picturing an organist playing a magnificent chord. He then lifts his hands from the organ, and the moments of silence that follow allow the chord to echo and "land" on the ears of those listening to it. To ponder is to let whatever you just experienced "land" within your mind and heart. So as we go to prayer today, let us first ask Mary for her help in pondering well.

Respond

1. How and where do you best "ponder in your heart" the things God is doing in your life?
2. How do you engage your mind in your pondering of God? How do you engage your heart?
3. Ask Mary to pray for you so that you can develop a receptive heart like hers.

FOURTH WEEK OF ADVENT

CHRISTMAS EVE

Return and Recollect

Again, we have an opportunity to pause from our daily rhythm to reflect on what the Lord has done in and for us this week. Think of this as the moment of collecting the gems you have mined this week in prayer and meditation. Instead of laboring ahead, let us pause and return to where we started to fully receive the gift of where we find ourselves today. While this might seem like an unnecessary repetition, be assured that pausing to look back is often when we discover the specific places and patterns God has been moving in throughout our prayer.

Return and Listen: Luke 2:8–20

Now there were shepherds in that region living in the fields and keeping the night watch over their flock. The angel of the Lord appeared to them and the glory of the Lord shone around them, and they were struck with great fear. The angel said to them, "Do not be afraid; for behold, I proclaim to you good news of great joy that will be for all the people. For today in the city of David a savior has been born for you who is Messiah and Lord. And this will be a sign for you: you will find an infant wrapped in swaddling clothes and lying in a manger." And suddenly there was a multitude of the heavenly host with the angel, praising God and saying:

"Glory to God in the highest
and on earth peace to those on whom his
favor rests."

When the angels went away from them to heaven, the shepherds said to one another, "Let us go, then, to Bethlehem to see this thing that has taken place, which the Lord has made known to us." So they went in haste and found Mary and Joseph, and the infant lying in the manger. When they saw this, they made known the message that had been told them about this child. All who heard it were amazed by what had been told them by the shepherds. And Mary kept all these things, reflecting on them in her heart. Then the shepherds returned, glorifying and praising God for all they had heard and seen, just as it had been told to them.

Return and Listen Again

Watch the animated video for "Shepherds, Keeping Watch," which can be found at the link below.

As you encounter the music and artwork again in a more dynamic way, consider how your journey of imaginative prayer through this week has brought this part of the story more to life for you. What has God revealed to you that you had never considered before? What details of the scriptures have come to the surface? What images now exist in your mind's eye when you read these words?

Scan this code with your phone or visit www.avemariapress.com/pages/way-of-the-star-resources to view animated art and music for "Shepherds, Keeping Watch."

Return and Respond

Collect your prayers from the week by reviewing your journaling notes and writing down anything that stands out to you. As you gather these "gems," pay attention to your own thoughts, feelings, and desires, and write down what you want to remember. Also record here any new observations, continuing questions, or answered prayers that you notice. Take them to Mass with you this evening or tomorrow, and present them on the altar during your Sunday worship. Even as you respond in your journal to everything you have experienced this week, try to remain in a posture of listening for the promptings of the Holy Spirit as you go.

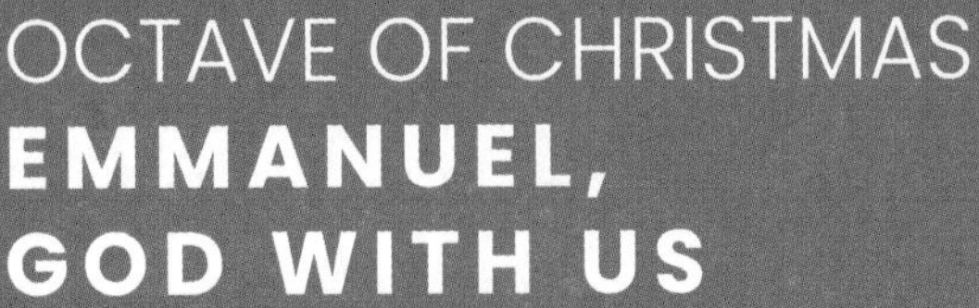
OCTAVE OF CHRISTMAS
EMMANUEL,
GOD WITH US

OCTAVE OF CHRISTMAS

CHRISTMAS DAY

Listen: Matthew 2:1–12

When Jesus was born in Bethlehem of Judea, in the days of King Herod, behold, magi from the east arrived in Jerusalem, saying, "Where is the newborn king of the Jews? We saw his star at its rising and have come to do him homage." When King Herod heard this, he was greatly troubled, and all Jerusalem with him. Assembling all the chief priests and the scribes of the people, he inquired of them where the Messiah was to be born. They said to him, "In Bethlehem of Judea, for thus it has been written through the prophet:

> 'And you, Bethlehem, land of Judah,
> are by no means least among the rulers
> of Judah;
> since from you shall come a ruler,
> who is to shepherd my people Israel.'"

Then Herod called the magi secretly and ascertained from them the time of the star's appearance. He sent them to Bethlehem and said, "Go and search diligently for the child. When you have found him, bring me word, that I too may go and do him homage." After their audience with the king they set out. And behold, the star that they had seen at its rising preceded them,

until it came and stopped over the place where the child was. They were overjoyed at seeing the star, and on entering the house they saw the child with Mary his mother. They prostrated themselves and did him homage. Then they opened their treasures and offered him gifts of gold, frankincense, and myrrh. And having been warned in a dream not to return to Herod, they departed for their country by another way.

Listen Again

Listen to "Emmanuel, God with Us," which can be found at the link below.

As you hear again many themes, melodies, and voices that you heard in previous passages, consider what each voice is saying to you in this moment as Jesus is born. Notice how the blend between the instruments—which have often signified interior movements of thoughts and emotions—strikes a balance with the human voices—which have often indicated the external voicing of thoughts and emotions. What particular meaning does this hold at this moment when the Messiah that has been held internally in Mary's womb is finally held externally in the arms of Mary and Joseph?

While you listen, look at the artwork at the beginning of this chapter and allow your imagination to draw you into the scene. Taking a hint from the music, draw from all the times throughout the Advent season that you spent imagining and meditating on

Scan this code with your phone or visit www.avemariapress.com/pages/way-of-the-star-resources **to find a video introduction to this week's prayer themes and a recording of "Emmanuel, God with Us."**

this story to inform what, who, and how you see as you experience this moment at the feet of Jesus in the manger.

Ponder: Red-Light Therapy and the Mystery of the Christ Child

Infrared saunas have made quite a splash in the health world in recent years. Among other things, red light is known for its healing qualities: It aids in reducing inflammation and increasing circulation and cell repair. Red-light bulbs, however, only mimic the original red light, which comes from the sun. Studies show that the sun naturally emits red light first thing in the morning. What astounds me is that you can gain benefits from this kind of sunlight just by being outside. You don't have to do anything else; your retina automatically takes in the light, and your body is affected.

This phenomenon speaks to the genius of God's creation. Simply by being in the presence of this healing light, we gain every benefit. It is estimated that only about 30 percent of this benefit reaches us through the glass of a window, so the full benefit is received only by standing outside with no barrier between us and the healing rays of God-given red-light therapy. There are many mornings, especially in the cold of winter, when I prefer to stay comfortably inside, but the ample benefit that comes from a brief time of discomfort usually compels me to endure the cold temperatures for at least a minute or two.

In this Christmas octave, we find ourselves at the foot of the manger, in the presence of Christ himself. The invitation this week is to move from meditation into adoration, even if it involves a degree of discomfort. Simply being in the presence of Jesus, the Light of the World who has come to save us, changes us on a spiritual cellular level.

Respond

1. In a very practical sense, how is God inviting you to continue and deepen the rhythm of prayer you've stepped into during this Advent?
2. To receive the light of Christ is also to reflect it. Where or to whom are you being called to carry the light of Christ during this Christmas season?
3. Approach Jesus with prayerful gratitude for his coming into the world—and into your life. If possible, visit an adoration chapel and spend a few minutes with him.

OCTAVE OF CHRISTMAS

DECEMBER 26

Listen: Matthew 2:1–2

When Jesus was born in Bethlehem of Judea, in the days of King Herod, behold, magi from the east arrived in Jerusalem, saying, "Where is the newborn king of the Jews? We saw his star at its rising and have come to do him homage." When King Herod heard this, he was greatly troubled, and all Jerusalem with him. Assembling all the chief priests and the scribes of the people, he inquired of them where the Messiah was to be born. They said to him, "In Bethlehem of Judea, for thus it has been written through the prophet:

'And you, Bethlehem, land of Judah,
are by no means least among the rulers
  of Judah;
since from you shall come a ruler,
who is to shepherd my people Israel.'"

Then Herod called the magi secretly and ascertained from them the time of the star's appearance. He sent them to Bethlehem and said, "Go and search diligently for the child. When you have found him, bring me word, that I too may go and do him homage." After their audience with the king they set out. And behold, the star that they had seen at its rising preceded them, until it came and stopped over the place where the child was. They were overjoyed at seeing the star, and on entering the house they saw the child with Mary his mother. They prostrated themselves and did him homage. Then they opened their treasures and offered him gifts of gold, frankincense, and myrrh. And having been warned in a dream not to return to Herod, they departed for their country by another way. (Mt 2:1–12)

Listen Again

As you begin to meditate on the bolded scripture above, engage your imagination and use the following questions to enter deeply into the scene. Had the people of Jerusalem noticed the star before the arrival of the Magi and wondered what it signified? When they arrive in Jerusalem, where do the Magi go to look for Jesus? Whom do they ask about his whereabouts? What kind of commotion does this cause in the streets of the city?

Ponder: The Cost of Following the Star

There is something so majestic about the journey of the Magi. As opposed to the shepherds, these men were known for their incredible social status, academic knowledge, and substantial wealth. We know they were astute in understanding matters of astronomy and astrology. In short, they were experts on the stars.

These high-society men traveled from afar—we all know the song that describes them crossing field and fountain, moor and mountain. But why? What were they searching for? "We saw his star at its rising and have come to do him homage," they said. They were following not just any star but "his" star.

To follow Jesus is a costly pursuit. He always gives back more than what he asks us to give, but we must recognize that the cost is real, and it requires a daily choice. This group of wise men, as we have come to call them, were pulled from their everyday lives to travel through some difficult terrain to pursue something higher that had gained their attention. They recognized that they were being drawn by the One whom the stars themselves obey, and their response was immediate and decisive.

Respond

1. In what ways has God captured your attention this Advent?
2. In what ways is he inviting you to brave the elements of your life in pursuit of something higher?
3. Ask God to inspire in you greater resolve and fortitude to follow where he is leading.

OCTAVE OF CHRISTMAS

DECEMBER 27

Listen: Matthew 2:3

When Jesus was born in Bethlehem of Judea, in the days of King Herod, behold, magi from the east arrived in Jerusalem, saying, "Where is the newborn king of the Jews? We saw his star at its rising and have come to do him homage." **When King Herod heard this, he was greatly troubled, and all Jerusalem with him.** Assembling all the chief priests and the scribes of the people, he inquired of them where the Messiah was to be born. They said to him, "In Bethlehem of Judea, for thus it has been written through the prophet:

'And you, Bethlehem, land of Judah,
are by no means least among the rulers
of Judah;
since from you shall come a ruler,
who is to shepherd my people Israel.'"

Then Herod called the magi secretly and ascertained from them the time of the star's appearance. He sent them to Bethlehem and said, "Go and search diligently for the child. When you have found him, bring me word, that I too may go and do him homage." After their audience with the king they set out. And behold, the star that they had seen at its rising preceded them,

until it came and stopped over the place where the child was. They were overjoyed at seeing the star, and on entering the house they saw the child with Mary his mother. They prostrated themselves and did him homage. Then they opened their treasures and offered him gifts of gold, frankincense, and myrrh. And having been warned in a dream not to return to Herod, they departed for their country by another way. (Mt 2:1–12)

Listen Again

As you begin to meditate on the bolded scripture above, engage your imagination and use the following questions to enter deeply into the scene. Imagine yourself present in the courts of King Herod's palace when the news of the Magi reaches him. How does King Herod receive the news? What is his reaction to the Magi and their search for a newborn king? Why is he troubled? Why is all Jerusalem also troubled by this news? Are the Magi surprised by the city's reaction to their arrival and message?

Ponder: Mary vs. King Herod

We are told that both Mary and King Herod were initially "troubled" at hearing the news of the coming of the Messiah. In the original text, the word used in both contexts is not exactly the same, but they are very closely related.

Mary and Herod both received the same news but had two very different responses. One chose trust, and the other chose suspicion. One chose surrender, and the other chose control. One chose to believe in Jesus's divine kingship, and the other chose to reject it.

When Mary chooses trust, surrender, and belief in the divine kingship of Jesus, she bears new life. When Herod chooses suspicion toward God, control, and rejection of Jesus as king, he literally brings death upon the Holy Innocents.

> By their fruits you will know them.
> —Matthew 7:16

Respond

1. Jesus came to share every aspect of life with us except sin, which means he is deeply present to each one of us, no matter the circumstances we face. How does that nearness challenge your faith? What parts of your life still need to be turned over to his kingship?
2. With deeper trust and surrender to Jesus's presence in your life, where is he calling you to go? What is he calling you to do?
3. Ask Mary to pray for you to welcome and surrender your life to God's will as she did.

OCTAVE OF CHRISTMAS

DECEMBER 28

Listen: Mathew 2:4–6

When Jesus was born in Bethlehem of Judea, in the days of King Herod, behold, magi from the east arrived in Jerusalem, saying, "Where is the newborn king of the Jews? We saw his star at its rising and have come to do him homage." When King Herod heard this, he was greatly troubled, and all Jerusalem with him. **Assembling all the chief priests and the scribes of the people, he inquired of them where the Messiah was to be born. They said to him, "In Bethlehem of Judea, for thus it has been written through the prophet:**

> **'And you, Bethlehem, land of Judah,**
> **are by no means least among the rulers**
> **of Judah;**
> **since from you shall come a ruler,**
> **who is to shepherd my people Israel.'"**

Then Herod called the magi secretly and ascertained from them the time of the star's appearance. He sent them to Bethlehem and said, "Go and search diligently for the child. When you have found him, bring me word, that I too may go and do him homage." After their audience with the king they set out. And behold, the star that they had seen at its rising preceded them,

until it came and stopped over the place where the child was. They were overjoyed at seeing the star, and on entering the house they saw the child with Mary his mother. They prostrated themselves and did him homage. Then they opened their treasures and offered him gifts of gold, frankincense, and myrrh. And having been warned in a dream not to return to Herod, they departed for their country by another way. (Mt 2:1–12)

Listen Again

As you begin to meditate on the bolded scripture above, engage your imagination and use the following questions to enter deeply into the scene. Imagine yourself again in the courts of King Herod as all the chief priests and scribes assemble to consult with him. Perhaps some are hopeful for the fulfillment of the prophecy, and others are trying to stifle it—how do you imagine the conversations unfolding? Is there a sense of confusion or competition? The experts in the room name Bethlehem as the birthplace of the new king—why does that startle or even terrify Herod, a man who has spent his life fighting to gain his kingdom? As you watch this moment unfold, what are your own thoughts, feelings, and desires that rise to the surface?

Ponder: Chiara Corbella Petrillo

It's a wonderful thing when the saints reveal themselves to us in heavenly friendship. I have had this happen a handful of times, and it is a delight and a true gift. A few years ago, I learned about the life of Servant of God Chiara Corbella Petrillo. It was as if she was spiritually tapping me on the shoulder for that exact time in my life.

Her story is worth looking up if you don't know it. Chiara had a particularly tumultuous vocational journey. She was dating her eventual husband, and during their courtship they broke up many times. The ups and downs of their relationship were a true suffering for her. One day, in her tumult, her spiritual director gave her a scripture verse that would change her trajectory.

> The holy one, the true,
> who holds the key of David,
> who opens and no one shall close,
> who closes and no one shall open.
> —Revelation 3:7

Chiara wrote that this line from Revelation changed her life. She was pierced to the heart with the reality that God is sovereign over all things—and that includes her own personal story. God's Word gave her confidence to surrender her life to him.

Today we hear of the fulfillment of a prophecy long foretold. Beyond what we can comprehend, God remains in complete control without violating an ounce of human free will. How far beyond us is the incredible might and mystery of God! On this fourth day of the Christmas octave, let us meditate on the concerns and joys that he is inviting us to lay down, and let us offer them along with the gifts of the Magi, trusting the dearest parts of our lives to God Almighty.

Respond

1. What areas of your life is God calling you to make a gift of to Jesus? How can you lay that part of yourself down before him as a gift as precious as what the Magi offered?
2. To whom do you turn for wisdom and guidance? Why are they trustworthy? What concerns weigh on your heart that might benefit from their insight?
3. In prayer, express your desire to let God rule your life, and ask him to help you where this feels difficult. Ask him to illuminate for you the areas you have yet to trust to him.

OCTAVE OF CHRISTMAS

DECEMBER 29

Listen: Matthew 2:7–8

When Jesus was born in Bethlehem of Judea, in the days of King Herod, behold, magi from the east arrived in Jerusalem, saying, "Where is the newborn king of the Jews? We saw his star at its rising and have come to do him homage." When King Herod heard this, he was greatly troubled, and all Jerusalem with him. Assembling all the chief priests and the scribes of the people, he inquired of them where the Messiah was to be born. They said to him, "In Bethlehem of Judea, for
thus it has been written through the prophet:

'And you, Bethlehem, land of Judah,
are by no means least among the rulers
of Judah;
since from you shall come a ruler,
who is to shepherd my people Israel.'"

Then Herod called the magi secretly and ascertained from them the time of the star's appearance. He sent them to Bethlehem and said, "Go and search diligently for the child. When you have found him, bring me word, that I too may go and do him homage." After their audience with the king they set out. And behold, the star that they had seen at its rising preceded them, until it came and stopped over the place where the child was. They were overjoyed at seeing the star, and on entering the house they saw the child with Mary his mother. They prostrated themselves and did him homage. Then they opened their treasures and offered him gifts of gold, frankincense, and myrrh. And having been warned in a dream not to return to Herod, they departed for their country by another way.

(Mt 2:1–12)

Listen Again

As you begin to meditate on the bolded scripture above, engage your imagination and use the following questions to enter deeply into the scene. Why does Herod call the Magi secretly? What is it like for the Magi to be called into the courts of the king? Do they feel a sense of honor or duty when given the charge to "search diligently for the child"? Why does Herod want to know the time of the star's appearance? What plans is he hatching, and what are his concerns?

Ponder: The Angel of Darkness Dressed as Light

St. Ignatius has a core teaching, and perhaps also a warning, about the angel of darkness dressed as light. The premise of this teaching is that Satan, being of high intellect as the angels are (even the fallen ones), is the great deceiver. We look back to the Garden of Eden, and we see that he tempts humanity not with overtly rotten fruit but with an apple that was "pleasing to the eyes" (Gn 3:6). At the start it looks really good, but we know that beneath the shiny skin of that apple lay the poison that would stain us.

King Herod is playing the same game here: He is trying to decipher Jesus's whereabouts under the guise of worshipping him when he really wants to destroy him. Herod is threatened by Jesus's kingship out of jealousy and a desire for power. Here at the start of Jesus's life, we see a foreshadowing of the very darkness that would take his life some thirty-three years later. While some accept his lordship and give him their lives in surrender and love, others reject him and seek to kill him.

The enemy prowls around like a roaring lion (1 Pt 5:8). The Magi model for us good discernment in recognizing the darkness in Herod's intentions. We, too, must be diligent in our daily discernment of where the angel of darkness is dressed as light and trying to lead us astray. As we advance in our intimacy with God through regular prayer, this growth will not go unopposed by the enemy, and he will use different disguises to distract us.

Respond

1. Are there any areas, situations, or relationships in your life where you are resisting or limiting the Lord? Is there anywhere you are moving in secret or trying to control his influence, perhaps out of fear? Bring those things specifically to him in prayer today.
2. In what ways have you faced spiritual opposition in your practice of prayer this Advent? How has that opposition appeared to you? What are effective ways for you to combat that temptation?
3. Ask the Holy Spirit to help you remain faithful in growing in your prayer life and to grant you clarity when you are being led astray.

OCTAVE OF CHRISTMAS

DECEMBER 30

Listen: Mathew 2:9

When Jesus was born in Bethlehem of Judea, in the days of King Herod, behold, magi from the east arrived in Jerusalem, saying, "Where is the newborn king of the Jews? We saw his star at its rising and have come to do him homage." When King Herod heard this, he was greatly troubled, and all Jerusalem with him. Assembling all the chief priests and the scribes of the people, he inquired of them where the Messiah was to be born. They said to him, "In Bethlehem of Judea, for thus it has been written through the prophet:

> 'And you, Bethlehem, land of Judah,
> are by no means least among the rulers
> of Judah;
> since from you shall come a ruler,
> who is to shepherd my people Israel.'"

Then Herod called the magi secretly and ascertained from them the time of the star's appearance. He sent them to Bethlehem and said, "Go and search diligently for the child. When you have found him, bring me word, that I too may go and do him homage." **After their audience with the king they set out. And behold, the star that they had seen at its rising preceded them,**

until it came and stopped over the place where the child was. They were overjoyed at seeing the star, and on entering the house they saw the child with Mary his mother. They prostrated themselves and did him homage. Then they opened their treasures and offered him gifts of gold, frankincense, and myrrh. And having been warned in a dream not to return to Herod, they departed for their country by another way. (Mt 2:1–12)

Listen Again

As you begin to meditate on the bolded scripture above, engage your imagination and use the following questions to enter deeply into the scene. What does the star look like as the Magi gaze upon it and follow it? What is the journey like for them as their eyes and imaginations are always drawn to the star? When the star stops over the place where Jesus is, what do they see? How does the place to which they are led align with or differ from their expectations?

Ponder: Westward Leading, Still Proceeding

Once upon a time, I found myself on a blind date with a great guy with whom I had several mutual friends. We had an immediate connection. Comparing notes later, neither of us thought we would click and were both caught off guard in the best way—a happy surprise.

There were some fundamental ideological differences between us, however, and shortly into dating we came to an impasse. We respected each other tremendously and ultimately wanted the best for the other. Both strong in our convictions, we ultimately went our separate ways. It was painful.

On the day we broke things off, he said something that stuck with me. He said, "Andrea, you know, I think right now we are like nearly parallel lines. The difference in degrees is small now, but over time we're going to end up in completely different places." Those words stung at the time, but I can see the wisdom in them now. If we are off in our trajectory by any small degree in our pursuit of something—especially something of great importance—over time we end up in a completely different place than we first intended.

This is an imperfect analogy, to be sure, but I think of this as I place myself on the journey with the Magi. It was important for them to follow the star that preceded them and to attend diligently to the direction they were receiving, not veering slightly in any other way. It was of the utmost importance to follow the signs correctly and move forward on the proper course; otherwise, they could end up in an entirely different place than at the feet of the baby Jesus.

Respond

1. How has God perfected and purified you in your journey of faith? Is he asking anything specific of you in terms of your vocation, your prayer life, your gifts, your circumstances, or your relationships?
2. What are the signs God has used to lead you in this season? How have you learned to attend to those signs?
3. In prayer, ask God to help you stay on course in the direction he has for your life.

OCTAVE OF CHRISTMAS

DECEMBER 31

Listen: Matthew 2:10–11

When Jesus was born in Bethlehem of Judea, in the days of King Herod, behold, magi from the east arrived in Jerusalem, saying, "Where is the newborn king of the Jews? We saw his star at its rising and have come to do him homage." When King Herod heard this, he was greatly troubled, and all Jerusalem with him. Assembling all the chief priests and the scribes of the people, he inquired of them where the Messiah was to be born. They said to him, "In Bethlehem of Judea, for thus it has been written through the prophet:

'And you, Bethlehem, land of Judah,
are by no means least among the rulers
of Judah;
since from you shall come a ruler,
who is to shepherd my people Israel.'"

Then Herod called the magi secretly and ascertained from them the time of the star's appearance. He sent them to Bethlehem and said, "Go and search diligently for the child. When you have found him, bring me word, that I too may go and do him homage." After their audience with the king they set out. And behold, the star that they had seen at its rising preceded them,

until it came and stopped over the place where the child was. **They were overjoyed at seeing the star, and on entering the house they saw the child with Mary his mother. They prostrated themselves and did him homage. Then they opened their treasures and offered him gifts of gold, frankincense, and myrrh.** And having been warned in a dream not to return to Herod, they departed for their country by another way. (Mt 2:1–12)

Listen Again

As you begin to meditate on the bolded scripture above, engage your imagination and use the following questions to enter deeply into the scene. What does the house beneath the star look like as the Magi arrive and enter? They experience a moment of being overjoyed—how is their joy met by that of Mary as she allows them to see and hold Jesus? For a simple carpenter and his humble wife, what is this moment like for Joseph to have noble men paying homage and offering gifts to their son?

Ponder: Holy Indifference

I have always been a fairly curious person—naturally inquisitive, you could say. As I read this gospel account and consider placing myself in the scene, I am taken aback by the variety of people who came to pay homage to the baby Jesus. We know Joseph and Mary were there, of course. We know the birth of Christ was announced first to the shepherds, who came barreling in from the fields, astounded at what they had seen and heard and then found that night. I wonder if the owner of the stable eventually came in to see the Holy Family. I wonder if the stable boy came to feed the animals, only to find a baby where he usually pours the food, in a beautiful Eucharistic foreshadowing (the artistry of God astounds me—it's all a wonder).

The exact timing of their visit is unknown, but we also know that at some point the Magi from the East made their way to Bethlehem. We've already concluded that the shepherds were men of low social pedigree, in contrast to the Magi's reputation, yet the Holy Family welcomes them all the same. In fact, as if to demonstrate God's equanimity in their encounters, the shepherds are elevated and the Magi bend a knee.

> The LORD makes poor and makes rich,
> humbles, and also exalts.
> —1 Samuel 2:7–8

St. Ignatius taught a concept called "holy indifference." He believed that we are all called to detachment from preference and to pursue a sole tethering to God and his holy will. I will admit, when I first heard this concept, I was not a fan. Or rather, in my initial misunderstanding of it, I was not a fan. Desires are good. They are holy. But Ignatius believed that ultimate freedom comes from indifference to whatever God allows in our lives: wealth or poverty, hiddenness or notoriety, singleness or marriage. In contrast to not caring, holy indifference is rather the disposition of saying yes and seeking beauty in the state of life God has led you to regardless—much easier said than done!

God remains always in control—he rules the whole universe, and he rules each of our lives. He is sovereign over all wealth, all social structure and status, all vocational callings. And he came that we all may have life and have it in abundance (Jn 10:10).

Respond

1. As we draw near to the end of this octave of Christmas, what is your interior disposition like? Which part of your heart life is Jesus inviting to rise up, to become elevated, emboldened?

In which part of your heart life is he inviting you to bend a knee and surrender to him?

2. What are the interior gifts you have received on this journey through Advent and Christmas? What gifts have you sought to give to Jesus?
3. Enter into reflective wonder and gratitude for the ways God has led you through this journey to follow the way of the star.

OCTAVE OF CHRISTMAS

JANUARY 1
SOLEMNITY OF MARY, MOTHER OF GOD

Listen: Matthew 2:12

When Jesus was born in Bethlehem of Judea, in the days of King Herod, behold, magi from the east arrived in Jerusalem, saying, "Where is the newborn king of the Jews? We saw his star at its rising and have come to do him homage." When King Herod heard this, he was greatly troubled, and all Jerusalem with him. Assembling all the chief priests and the scribes of the people, he inquired of them where the Messiah was to be born. They said to him, "In Bethlehem of Judea, for thus it has been written through the prophet:

'And you, Bethlehem, land of Judah,
are by no means least among the rulers
of Judah;
since from you shall come a ruler,
who is to shepherd my people Israel.'"

Then Herod called the magi secretly and ascertained from them the time of the star's appearance. He sent them to Bethlehem and said, "Go and search diligently for the child. When you have found him, bring me word, that I too may go and do him homage." After their audience with the king they set out. And behold, the star that they had seen at its rising preceded them, until it came and stopped over the place where the child was. They were overjoyed at seeing the star, and on entering the house they saw the child with Mary his mother. They prostrated themselves and did him homage. Then they opened their treasures and offered him gifts of gold, frankincense, and myrrh. **And having been warned in a dream not to return to Herod, they departed for their country by another way.** (Mt 2:1–12)

Listen Again

As you begin to meditate on the bolded scripture above, engage your imagination and use the following questions to enter deeply into the scene. Where do the Magi sleep? Do they all have the same dream? How do they receive the warning not to return to Herod? Do they share any of this warning with Mary and Joseph? When they depart by another way, what new challenges emerge for their journey? When they reach their homeland, do they proclaim Jesus to those in their community?

Ponder: By Another Way (A Final Listening)

We come now to the final moment of reflection from our Advent and Christmas journey. Like the Saturdays during Advent, we invite you to a final listening. But instead of just looking back at one week, look back over your notes from the past four Saturdays to find the highlights of your journey through this season.

What has the Lord revealed to you in these last weeks? What consistent themes do you see woven like a golden thread throughout the journey the Lord has led you on? There could be some surprising insights he wants to communicate to you. The gems are indeed worth mining! As a helpful tip, consider using a different color pen from the one you have been journaling with and underline or circle the portions that stick out in your review.

As a final exhortation, I'd like to offer you this: Encountering Jesus Christ changes us. After the Magi encountered the Christ Child, we are told that "they departed for their country by another way." As we leave this Advent season and Christmas octave, our lives have been set on a different trajectory—we have the invitation before us to walk the path of faith in a different way from when we started together and to return to our lives by a new way.

> Oh, Jesus, in your mercy and love, give us eyes to see, ears to hear, and a heart that knows you. Give us the grace to live differently after encountering you. Amen.

Respond

Watch the animated video for "Emmanuel, God with Us," which can be found at the link below.

As you encounter the music and artwork again in a more dynamic way, consider how your journey of imaginative prayer through this week has brought this part of the story more to life for you. What has God revealed to you that you had never considered before? What details of the scriptures have come to the surface? What images now exist in your mind's eye when you read these words?

Scan this code with your phone or visit www.avemariapress.com/pages/way-of-the-star-resources to view animated art and music for "Emmanuel, God with Us."

Review your journaling notes from this book. How has this Advent and Christmas journey changed you? What reflections or insights has God revealed to you in prayer? What "golden threads" do you discover as you look over your journaling?

Record here any observations, answered prayers, continuing questions, or deepened desires you notice. Take them to Mass with you this evening or tomorrow, and present them on the altar during your Sunday worship.

The Vigil Project is a nonprofit apostolate founded in 2016 by a community of music artists united in a vision to restore excellence in Catholic music and invite Catholics into deeper encounter with God. Focused on music for devotional prayer and parish ministry, the Vigil Project has released ten studio albums, has toured hundreds of parishes across the United States and Europe, and will soon release a first-of-its-kind documentary film series, *Meaning of Music*.

In 2025, the Vigil Project led the International Summit for Catholic Musicians in Italy, bringing together musicians from a dozen countries for prayer and formation. Through its music, events, and resources, the apostolate remains dedicated to excellence, innovation, and creativity in service of the Gospel.

The Vigil Project team is based in New Orleans, Louisiana; South Bend, Indiana; and Cincinnati, Ohio.

Learn more at thevigilproject.com.

Andrea Thomas is cofounder of the Vigil Project. She studied vocal performance at Belmont University and, during her freshman year, auditioned for the *VeggieTales Live!* stage production, earning a lead role that took her on a one-hundred-show tour.

She later transferred to Franciscan University of Steubenville, where she earned a bachelor's degree in theology with minors in marketing and finance. After graduation, she held university positions in development and conference planning. Desiring a greater sense of community as well as music for her own life of devotion, she collaborated with other musicians on a project for Lent and Easter that later became the foundation of the Vigil Project.

Thomas has recorded more than a dozen studio albums and toured throughout the United States and Europe, passionate about helping people encounter God through the beauty of music.

She resides in Cincinnati, Ohio.

Greg Boudreaux is cofounder of the Vigil Project. His love for sacred music began in childhood, watching his mother lead music at Mass.

After graduating from Auburn University with a bachelor's degree in business management, he discerned a call to full-time music ministry and worked with numerous apostolates, providing music for events centered on Eucharistic encounters. After marrying his wife, Lizzy, the couple formed a musical duo, released two albums, and toured nationally, sharing the Theology of the Body through song and personal testimony.

In 2016, weary from the road, they collaborated with friends on a collection of songs for Lent and Easter that later became the foundation of the Vigil Project.

Boudreaux resides in Covington, Louisiana, with Lizzy and their children.

Natalie Haydel Barker is the artist for *Way of the Star* by the Vigil Project. She is the founder of Colors by Natalie, a creative brand known for its vibrant abstract artwork and custom commissions.

Discover more of her work at colorsbynatalie.art.